Reading as Rhetorical Invention

College Section Committee

Reading as Rhetorical Invention

Knowledge, Persuasion, and the Teaching of Research-Based Writing

Doug Brent
University of Calgary

National Council of Teachers of English
1111 Kenyon Road, Urbana, Illinois 61801

Manuscript Editor: William Tucker

Interior Design: Tom Kovacs for TGK Design

Cover Design: Doug Burnett

NCTE Stock Number 38500–3050

Library of Congress Cataloging-in-Publication Data

Brent, Doug.
    Reading as rhetorical invention: knowledge, persuasion, and the teaching of research-based writing / Doug Brent.
        p. cm.
    Revision of the author's thesis.
    Includes bibliographical references and index.
    ISBN 0-8141-3850-0
    1. English language—Rhetoric—Study and teaching. 2. Reading (Higher education) 3. Persuasion (Rhetoric) I. Title.
PE 1404.B73 1992
808'.0427'07—dc20   91–44001
                                                                          CIP

The Electric Monk was a labour-saving device, like a dishwasher or a video recorder. Dishwashers washed tedious dishes for you, thus saving you the bother of washing them yourself, video recorders watched tedious television for you, thus saving you the bother of looking at it yourself; Electric Monks believed things for you, thus saving you what was becoming an increasingly onerous task, that of believing all the things the world expected you to believe. Unfortunately this Electric Monk had developed a fault, and had started to believe all kinds of things, more or less at random.
—Douglas Adams, *Dirk Gently's Holistic Detective Agency*

Contents

Acknowledgments

One of the main theses of this book is that you can never fully identify the incomprehensible number of people who contribute, directly or indirectly, to the making of any text. However, certain voices in the unending conversation stand out more than others, and I would particularly like to thank Jo Powell and Andrea Lunsford for their support and suggestions. I am most especially indebted to Nan Johnson, who supervised the original version of this material as a doctoral dissertation and who insisted on nothing but the best.

I would also like to acknowledge the support and encouragement of my wife, Diana Brent, and the patience of my children Kimberley and Heather, who have done without large portions of my attention for the past several years.

Preface

Why does rhetoric need a theory of reading? Neither teachers nor theoreticians have ever seriously doubted that reading and writing are intimately connected. In the past decade in particular, teachers of both reading and composition have generated a torrent of books and articles that attempt to trace the connections between reading and writing skills and to suggest exactly how training in one can be used to improve skill in the other. At the same time, from a more philosophical perspective, rhetorical theorists have been intensely exploring the connection from a different angle: the relationships between discourse and knowledge. The classical Western, or Graeco-Roman, view that certain types of contingent truth can best be uncovered through debate has expanded into the view that all forms of truth can exist only through social interaction. "Reading and writing connections" has become a particular case of the more general principle that all our knowledge—not just what we choose to write down but everything that forms our personalities—is created by interaction with other communicating selves. Rhetoric, we can now say with as much conviction as we are allowed in such matters, is not just a communicative but also an epistemic process.

Philosophers such as Thomas Kuhn and Michael Polanyi argue that knowledge, even the most "scientific" knowledge, is not made simply through individual encounters with the physical world. Rather, knowledge exists as a consensus of many individual knowers, a consensus that is negotiated through the medium of discourse in an unending conversation that involves all humanity.[1] Rhetoric interpenetrates every aspect of this conversation. If knowledge is negotiated, it follows that differing views are involved in a competition for the minds of believers. Knowledge is not simply what one has been told. Knowledge is what one *believes*, what one accepts as being at least provisionally true. Symbolic negotiation is thus a process in which competing propositions attempt to establish claims to be worth believing. Only when such a claim is established can a proposition be elevated to the status of knowledge.

In short, then, persuasion, the essence of rhetoric, lies at the heart of this endlessly recursive process of producing and consuming discourse. Modern rhetoricians such as Wayne Booth and Kenneth Burke have developed rhetorics that take account of this belief that rhetoric is epistemic—that it participates not just in the conveying of knowledge already formulated but also in the making of knowledge through symbolic interaction.[2] This view of rhetoric implies that the reception of discourse through hearing or reading is also epistemic. To attend to a discourse is not simply to absorb another person's meanings. It is also to participate in the creation of new knowledge through the process of symbolic negotiation.

It is this shift in rhetorical philosophy that has made the status of "reading-writing connections" so much more than a practical matter. On the face of it, rhetoric and reading seem to be related, but separate, arts. Rhetoric is the art of discourse seen from the producer's point of view; its function is to show a speaker or writer how to develop and manage arguments, arrangement, and style in order to persuade an audience. Reading, on the other hand, is the art of discourse seen from the consumer's point of view. The function of a theory of reading is to show a reader how to interpret discourse in order to understand and use what a writer has produced. But if the production of all knowledge is an intensely social process, then we should be able to describe in some detail exactly *how* the process of taking in others' ideas through reading relates to the process, separable from the first in name only, of devising arguments that will persuade others.

This is why rhetorical theory must be revised to include a theory of reading. Given the modern epistemological framework, we can no longer ask the question of how one can persuade others without asking the equally rhetoric-based question of how one is persuaded by others' arguments. For reading is not simply a matter of "taking in" others' ideas. The bubbling rhetorical stew in which we are all immersed from birth presents us with a mass of opinions about everything from the ethicality of abortion to the composition of the moon's core or the price of eggs. We know from experience that some of these opinions will be inappropriate for us or simply wrong. Many will be mutually contradictory. The process of building a set of beliefs about our world, a set of beliefs that combines matters of the highest import with those of the most total triviality, must involve deciding *which* of these babbling voices to believe, and with what degree of conviction.

This book seeks to build a model of how we rhetorical beings accomplish this task. In particular, it seeks to build a model of rhetorical invention premised on the idea that reading—that is, being persuaded by other people's texts—is a vital component of rhetorical invention, for it is an important way of participating in the conversation that gives us all of our meanings. In short, it will explore the implications of expanding rhetoric to take account of the social view of knowledge.

This inquiry encloses a number of more specific and closely related subquestions:

1. What aspects of rhetoric, both traditional and modern, can inform a theory of rhetorical reading?
2. How can we describe within a rhetorical framework how meaning is generated during the act of reading? That is, how does a reader know what propositions a writer is trying to persuade her to believe?
3. How does a reader evaluate the propositions presented by individual texts and decide which to be persuaded by?
4. How does a reader negotiate among the claims of various texts in order to develop a unified system of knowledge?

The search for answers to these questions will obviously take us into reading theory as well as into rhetorical theory. Literary criticism, particularly reader-response criticism, has long been asking very similar questions from its own point of view. So has cognitive science, which seeks by more empirical methods to develop a model of non-aesthetic reading as a cognitive process. By recasting the insights of these two disciplines in an explicitly rhetorical framework, we can begin to understand how the reciprocal processes of reading and writing function together to produce knowledge.

The answers to these questions can provide a new view of a number of related activities. At the most practical, teacherly level, it can help us understand what we are doing when we teach students how to write papers based on research. As I will argue in more detail later, the "research paper" is one of the most important forms of academic writing. In the composition class, it typically occurs as a poorly understood, rather orphaned form when it appears at all. My own early attempts to teach students to write papers based on research were fraught with a profound sense of failure. My students learned how to use quotations, more or less: that is, they learned how many spaces to indent and on which side of the quotation marks to place the period. They learned how to find information in the library and how to document it when they used it. But their research papers, by and large, remained hollow imitations of research, collections of information gleaned from sources with little evaluation, synthesis, or original thought. They approached research as they would gathering shells at the beach, picking up ideas with interesting colors or unusual shapes and putting them in a bucket without regard for overall pattern. I was tempted to dismiss the research process as unteachable.

Yet research, when liberated from its ghetto in Week 7 of freshman composition, is the main mode of developing thought in academic disciplines, including our own. Like us, students develop their familiarity with a discipline by reading the discourse of that discipline and then committing to paper the knowledge that they have developed with the help of their reading. In its broadest definition, "research" simply means making contact with other human beings by reading the texts they have produced, and then updating one's own system of beliefs with reference to those texts. It represents a particularly social form of inquiry, a form of inquiry in which the reader/writer attends consciously both to the others that inform his discourse—his sources—and the others that will receive it—his audience. It is, in fact, the classroom version of the way in which virtually all human knowledge is rhetorically developed.

Yet few of us in the academic world—embarrassingly, rhetoricians perhaps least of all—really understand how to help students make the incredibly difficult choice of *what to believe* from the masses of contradictory information they read. Long before we worry about teaching them the conventions of note taking and documentation, we (meaning all who find ourselves teaching writing, whether in composition classes or in history, sociology, or biochemistry) should be helping them acquire this astonishingly complex and difficult skill. Charles Bazerman, one of the earliest theorists to recognize the conversational nature of disciplinary writing, insists that

> If as teachers of writing we want to prepare our students to enter into the written interchanges of their chosen disciplines and the various discussions of personal and public interest, we must cultivate various techniques of absorbing, reformulating, commenting on, and using reading.[3]

To do that, we need to understand what this skill *is*. I will turn to this practical application of the theory in the final chapter.

A rhetorical model of reading can also inform rhetorical criticism. By enlarging and defining the theoretical horizons of both reading theory and rhetorical theory, such a model can enable a more complex discussion of the relationships among texts. A concern with intertextuality is not new to rhetorical criticism, but most rhetorical criticism of an intertextual nature concentrates on linguistic echoes—borrowings of phrases, tropes, stock appeals. Such analyses are not intended to account in detail for the ways in which writers' participation in a larger conversation builds their beliefs as well as their language structures. By examining texts from the point of view of a larger rhetorical conversation, we can focus not just on relationships between persuasive techniques, but also on relationships between the propositions argued by texts in the context of rhetorical inquiry. In other words, we can not only look at why a particular author phrases her arguments in just such a way; we can also inquire into the development of the ideas themselves. This entails a focus on the ways in which different authors appear to interpret the same written sources in different ways, thereby suggesting how particular configurations of personal beliefs, goals, and prior knowledge influence the reading process. In short, then, the rhetorical analysis of texts can be refocused from a description of persuasive methods to a description of the ways in which beliefs are constructed and negotiated in discourse. Thus is born a subspecies of rhetorical criticism that I will call "dialogic criticism."

Finally, an understanding of how reading and rhetoric fit together has implications much more general than textual analysis or composition teaching. In *The Pursuit of Signs*, Jonathan Culler argues that the study of literature should be more than a mere piling-up of interpretations: "To engage in the study of literature is not to produce yet another interpretation of *King Lear* but to advance one's understanding of the conventions and operations of an institution, a mode of discourse."[4] The same can be said for a rhetorical analysis of reading. It is not simply a means of understanding particular ways in which people read or fail to; it is also a means of understanding one of the primary mechanisms of understanding itself.

If we can advance our understanding of the conventions and operations of reading as a rhetorical mode of building belief, we may be able to advance our understanding of the divisions in society that result from diversity of belief. It is always dangerous to claim that a new theoretical perspective can make sweeping changes in the conduct of our lives. The everyday world has a way of turning as before, apparently ignoring the implications of new theories about how it does so. But it is nonetheless tempting to speculate that if we can understand the sources of division in society we may be better able to heal them. In *Modern Dogma and the Rhetoric of Assent*, Wayne Booth sets such a goal for rhetoric:

> If it is good for men to attend to each others' reasons--and we all know that it is, for without such attending none of us could come to be and questions about value could not even be asked--it is also good to work for whatever conditions make such mutual inquiry possible.[5]

This is a lofty goal indeed. But perhaps by increasing our understanding of how beliefs are formed through reading—that is, of one of the conditions that make mutual inquiry possible—a rhetoric of reading may help us work to improve those conditions.

Notes

1. See Thomas S. Kuhn, *The Structure of Scientific Revolutions*, 2nd ed. (Chicago: University of Chicago Press, 1970), and Michael Polanyi, *Personal Knowledge: Towards a Post-Critical Philosophy* (Chicago: University of Chicago Press, 1958).

2. See Wayne C. Booth, *Modern Dogma and the Rhetoric of Assent* (Chicago: University of Chicago Press, 1974), and Kenneth Burke, *The Philosophy of Literary Form* (Berkeley: University of California Press, 1941).

3. Charles Bazerman, "A Relationship between Reading and Writing: The Conversational Model," *College English*, 41 (1980): 658.

4. Jonathan Culler, *The Pursuit of Signs: Semiotics, Literature, Deconstruction* (Ithaca: Cornell University Press, 1981), 5.

5. Booth, 137.

1 Starting Points

The Traditional Framework

Consuming and producing discourse are inseparable and reciprocal acts; neither is logically subordinate to the other. However, because I intend to view both activities in the context of persuasion—of both persuading through and being persuaded by discourse—the art of rhetoric can be considered superordinate to both. From its inception, rhetoric has codified the mechanisms of human persuasion, and it is under the heading of rhetoric that we can most conveniently gather the persuasive aspects of both reading and writing.

Let us begin, then, with the first of the four questions posed in the preface: "What aspects of rhetoric, both traditional and modern, can inform a theory of rhetorical reading?" This is essentially a question of definition; it is a way of asking "What exactly is a *rhetorical* view of reading, as opposed to any other view of reading?" To put the question another way, what can we learn by placing the act of reading in a larger rhetorical context that we cannot learn from studying reading as a separate act?

To understand what it means to read rhetorically, we must first identify the essential features of rhetoric itself. Perhaps the most fundamental defining feature of rhetoric is that articulated by Aristotle when he defines rhetoric as "the faculty of discovering in the particular case what are the available means of persuasion."[1] This definition, however, is helpful only if we can, in turn, define persuasion. As George Kennedy suggests, the classical concept of "persuasion" carried a considerable range of meaning:

> The ancient world commonly thought of this purpose [i.e., the purpose of rhetoric] as persuasion, but meant by that something much looser and more inclusive than persuasion as understood by a modern social scientist. Purposes cover a whole spectrum from converting hearers to a view opposed to that they previously held, to implanting a conviction not otherwise considered, to the deepening of belief in a view already favorably entertained, to a demonstration of the cleverness of the author, to teaching or exposition.[2]

1

Aristotle himself gives no formal definition of the term, but from the types of speeches that he discusses under the heading of rhetoric, we can determine the range of acts that he considered persuasive—that is, rhetorical. For Aristotle, "persuasion" could mean inducing an audience to act, as in a speech intended to convince Athenians to declare war or build new ships. But it could also mean simply inducing the audience to believe something, as in a speech intended to convince an audience that a particular man is honorable or dishonorable, guilty or not guilty. Thus classical rhetoric was not limited to attempts to induce overt action by the audience.

This broad use of the term "persuasion" has been reaffirmed by modern rhetoricians. In *Rhetorical Dimensions in Criticism*, for instance, Donald C. Bryant defines rhetoric as "the rationale of the informative and suasory in discourse." This definition, according to Bryant,

> implies two distinguishable but closely entangled dimensions of discourse as rhetorical, and it implies others which are not. Perhaps it dodges or circumvents the problems of genre, but I think rather that it recognizes pure genres as fictions and implies that most artifacts of discourse exhibit various dimensions, the informative-suasory of which comprise the province of rhetoric.[3]

By using a compound term such as "informative-suasory," Bryant acknowledges that it is impossible to reliably distinguish discourse intended to change belief from discourse intended to prompt action. To persuade a person to act, you must persuade her to believe that the proposed action is good or desirable; to convince her of a proposition, you must persuade her to treat it as being true. Thus persuasion can be seen at the heart of even the most apparently neutral informative discourse. Such discourse is an attempt to persuade the audience to alter, if ever so slightly, their beliefs as to the way the world is or ought to be.

This does not, of course, mean that there is never a motive for making a rough distinction between discourse that is overtly persuasive and discourse that is not. Many useful taxonomies, such as Kinneavy's influential (if controversial) *A Theory of Discourse*, are founded on exactly this distinction. However, it is also true that "persuasion" can be seen as a vital defining feature of rhetoric without limiting rhetoric to discourse that seeks to influence overt behavior.

This is an important point, for the sort of reading that I am attempting to place in a rhetorical context—reading to build a system of beliefs based on response to other people's texts—frequently does not appear to involve overtly "persuasive" texts at all. The reader is often consciously seeking information, not attitude change, and may confine her search entirely to apparently objective works that seek as much as possible to keep the writer's opinions out of the transaction with the reader. Yet even the most coldly informative written discourse presents not just information but a certain worldview, a complex of beliefs held, or presented as being held, by the author. A description of the digestive organs of a frog is not a transparent window on reality but a description of reality as the author believes it to be—even if it is such a basic description of sensory data that there is absolutely no reason to dispute it. Reading such discourse involves not simply a passive uptake of information, but the act of accepting as true the view of reality presented. This acceptance results at least in part from the suasory power of the discourse. Thus, reading is an active attempt to find in discourse that which one can be persuaded is at least provisionally true, that which contains elements worth adding to one's own worldview. A rhetoric of reading must therefore account not just for the way a reader decodes meanings from texts, but also how she decides what meanings to accept, what meanings to be persuaded by.

Once we have defined rhetorical reading as reading that broadly seeks to persuade a reader to accept certain propositions as worth believing, other features naturally follow. Defining rhetoric as the art of influencing behavior and belief implies a faith that discourse is a reasonably reliable means by which one person can affect another. If discourse has no power to connect rhetor and audience, persuasion can have no meaning. But discourse must do more than simply communicate; it must enable the rhetor to control the responses of the audience in more or less predictable ways. This further entails a faith that there are at least a few assumptions about human nature that can be treated as generally true. Otherwise, it would be impossible to predict human response with any degree of accuracy.

This belief in predictability does not necessarily mean that the rhetor exerts complete control over his audience. In the *Gorgias*, Plato satirizes this extreme sophistic view in Polus's claim that rhetors can "act like tyrants and put to death anyone they please and confiscate property and banish anyone they've a mind to."[4] Plato's Socrates, as always, easily demolishes this claim. Plato does, however, acknowledge a connection between the form and content of a discourse and its effect; as he points out in the *Phaedrus*, the competent rhetorician must "discover the kind of speech that matches each type of nature" and then use this information to evoke the desired response from his audience.[5] Aristotle's more practical rhetoric develops this idea in more detail, showing how one's arguments must be chosen according to whether the audience is young or old, rich or poor, friendly or unfriendly. Today, after twenty-five centuries of largely unsuccessful attempts to develop algorithms to predict behavior, we might be more cautious about such generalizations. Yet behind even the most cautious attempts to suggest what will and will not affect an audience lies a basic assumption that underpins all rhetorical precepts: human beings act not at random, but rather for reasons that the rhetor can predict and use. This assumption can never be fully abandoned if rhetoric is to be true to its mandate as an art of persuasion.

A rhetorical view of reading, however, must deal with more than the basic "rhetorical triangle" of a rhetor connected to an audience by a text. Rhetoric involves discovering not just the means of persuasion, but the means of persuasion (as Aristotle puts it) "in the particular case." This implies that rhetoric must be able to account for the ways in which means of persuasion vary not just with the rhetor and the audience, but also according to where the speech is being presented, for what reason, and under what circumstances.

For Aristotle, this requirement generated a division of rhetoric into three specific kinds: forensic (legal), deliberative (political), and epideictic (ceremonial). These divisions are no longer appropriate, for modern society provides far more diverse opportunities for rhetorical discourse than did the classical world. However, as Lloyd Bitzer reminds us in "The Rhetorical Situation," rhetoric must still take account of the occasion in the form of the exigency, which Bitzer defines as "a defect, an obstacle, something waiting to be done, a thing which is other than it should be."[6] Rhetoric is not just persuasion in the abstract, but persuasion designed to bring about a change in a specific aspect of the surrounding context. A rhetorical theory of reading, then, must also take account of the context of the act of persuasion.

In addition to asking what features a rhetorical theory of reading must have in order to be rhetorical by definition, we must ask what additional features are suggested by the rhetorical framework that may help to illuminate the process. That is, once rhetorical reading is defined as a means by which the reader is persuaded, what does that suggest about how we can describe it?

Along with the general definition of rhetoric as an art of persuasion and the assumptions thereby entailed, traditional rhetoric supplies some more or less standard terms for discussing the means of persuasion. These terms are not sufficiently universal to be written into a definition of rhetoric. However, they are so commonly associated with rhetoric that we can reasonably expect them, or at least the ways of seeing that they imply, to influence any art qualif: ed by the term "rhetorical."

One of the most fundamental of these sets of terms is the division of the means of persuasion into categories. The most useful and enduring of these categories are the Aristotelian modes of proof: logos, pathos, and ethos; that is, proof by reasoned argument, by appeals to the emotions of the audience, and by reference to the character of the speaker. The relative emphasis placed on these modes has, like the relative emphasis placed on form and matter, varied over the ages. But it is a fundamental postulate of the art of rhetoric that, regardless of their relative merits, there are different modes of appeal: that human nature is not unitary, and appeals can be profitably classed according to the aspects of human nature to which they refer.

Terminology, as Kenneth Burke points out, is not just a reflection of reality, but a way of seeing, a way of making distinctions that would be made differently if a different terminology were employed.[7] By pressing the act of reading to see if it will yield some of the distinctions suggested by the language of traditional rhetoric, we can highlight those features that are the most specifically rhetorical; that is, those features that are the most tied to rhetoric's grounding in persuasion. The traditional distinction between the modes of proof will lead us to investigate the degree to which psychological processes other than pure intellection are involved in deciding what meanings to be persuaded by. How can ethos, the speaker's character, play a significant role in reading a text whose author is not physically present? What place does pathos, the emotional reaction to a text and the propositions presented by it, have in the building of a belief system based on written sources?

Traditional rhetoric thus plays two related roles in a rhetoric of reading. First, it plays a definitional role. The traditional definition of rhetoric itself sets an irreducible minimum of features that a rhetoric of reading must have if it is to merit its label as a branch of rhetorical investigation. It must account for reading as more than merely a transaction between text and reader. It must account for reading as a transaction between writer and audience by means of a text. This in turn implies that there is some connection, however tenuous, between the meaning the writer intends and the meaning the reader interprets the text as having. Whether or not it actively focuses on the problem of intentionality, any theory of reading that calls itself rhetorical must account for interpretation in a way that allows for this deliberate transfer of meaning.

Second, it plays a heuristic role. We need not be bound by the terminology it supplies, but using that terminology to the greatest extent possible directs our attention to certain distinctions and raises certain questions that might not be asked, or not asked as directly, by a theory of reading that is not explicitly situated in a rhetorical framework. In short, then, once we see reading as a process of persuasion that falls under the superordinate term of "rhetoric," we have a powerful set of tools with which to limit and direct the investigation of the process.

Rhetoric in a Constructionist Age

I have sketched the features of traditional rhetoric that separate a rhetoric of reading from any other theory of how texts are interpreted; however, I have not yet explained why such an account is needed. What is it about the process of producing and consuming discourse that demands that it be accounted for by a seemingly oxymoronic "rhetoric of reading," when the two separate arts have provided satisfactory accounts for twenty-five centuries?

The reason is that rhetoric is now seen not just as a tool for transmitting ideas and persuading others to believe them, but also as a communal medium in which thought grows. This change reflects a shift in overall focus: rather than concentrating on the specific task of composing a piece of discourse that will persuade the audience to accept the rhetor's propositions, many modern rhetoricians concentrate on the larger issue of how rhetoric is part of a dialectical process of developing new knowledge by discussion. This shift in focus makes a rhetoric of reading both more possible and more necessary than in the traditional framework, and also suggests additional features of the rhetorical transaction that a rhetoric of reading must account for.

This view of rhetoric is rooted in an all-encompassing shift in the theory of knowledge itself. One of the earliest and still one of the most influential proponents of the new epistemology, Thomas Kuhn, argues in *The Structure of Scientific Revolutions* that scientific "knowledge" is not objective knowledge of a real natural world.[8] Although he never argues that there is no such thing as an objective universe, he claims that our knowledge of that universe is subjective and is held communally by groups of scientists who speak the same language, attach the same meaning to scientific terminology, and operate within the same assumptions about what a valid problem is and what are valid ways of solving it. These communities of thought, which Kuhn calls "paradigms" or "disciplinary matrices," are constituted linguistically. A new paradigm arises when a scientist or group of scientists, having developed a theory that appears to account for reality better than old theories did, convinces other scientists to adopt it, and thereby creates a new thought community. Although he never explicitly uses the word "rhetoric," then, Kuhn, in fact, is constructing a rhetorically based epistemology. Scientific knowledge, for Kuhn, is socially constructed by a process of mutual persuasion.

Michael Polanyi, also a philosopher of science, makes this rhetorical view of epistemology even more explicit. In *Personal Knowledge*, Polanyi notes that knowledge cannot continue to exist without being shared:

> In order to be satisfied, our intellectual passions must find response. This universal intent creates a tension: we suffer when a vision of reality to which we have committed ourselves is contemptuously ignored by others. For a general unbelief imperils our own convictions by evoking an echo in us. Our vision must conquer or die.[9]

Thus arises what Polanyi calls the "persuasive passion": the drive to solidify one's own beliefs by persuading others to share them.

Not all social constructionist epistemologies take such a rhetorical focus, even implicitly. For example, in "The Voice of Poetry in the Conversation of Mankind," Michael Oakeshott argues that we participate in a never-ending conversation whose primary role is not inquiry but simply conversation itself: "Of course there is argument and inquiry and information, but wherever these are profitable they are to be recognized as passages in this conversation, and perhaps they are not the most captivating of the passages."[10] This may well be true, but for our purposes here, the passages of argument and inquiry are by far the most captivating, for they are the passages in which human beings seek to build beliefs through conscious inquiry into the beliefs of others.

Wayne Booth's rhetoric is a particularly good example of social construction viewed through an explicitly rhetorical lens. In *Modern Dogma and the Rhetoric of Assent*, Booth argues for a rhetoric that can explain how we acquire knowledge other than through totally objective science or totally subjective values (the "modern dogma" of his title). For Booth, knowledge is not something discovered by the isolated self in its interaction with the physical world. Rather, knowledge arises through interaction between selves. Booth begins with a proposition that, he argues, everyone in fact operates under in practice even if they say that they don't believe it: "It is reasonable to grant (one *ought* to grant) some degree of credence to whatever qualified men and women agree on."[11] From this starting point, he develops a communal view of knowledge in which one knows the world "through a willing assent to the process of making an intelligible world with my fellow creatures."[12] Profoundly affected by Polanyi's work, Booth argues that even scientific knowledge is constructed socially:

> This is in formal structure—as Michael Polanyi among others has shown—the process of validation used even by scientists for a great share of their scientific beliefs. No scientist has ever performed experiments or calculations providing more than a tiny fraction of all the scientific beliefs he holds; the whole edifice of science depends on faith in witnesses, past and present—on testimony and tradition....
>
> Thus science is, in its larger structures, validated by the same social processes that I am arguing for in "all the rest."[13]

This view of knowledge is intimately connected with a view of the self. For Booth, the self is not an isolated entity that finds knowledge of facts through individual interaction with nature and knowledge of values through individual probing of itself. Rather, the self is "a field of selves":

> It is *essentially* rhetorical, symbol exchanging, a social product in process of changing through interaction, sharing values with other selves. Even when thinking privately, "I" can never escape the other selves which I have taken in to make "myself," and my thought will thus always be a dialogue.[14]

This use of the term "rhetoric" for this process of building a world through symbolic interaction dramatically extends the meaning of the term. Under Booth's definition, rhetoric is not merely an art of persuasion. It is "a whole philosophy of how men succeed or fail in discovering together, in discourse, new levels of truth (or at least agreement) that neither suspected before."[15] Yet this reshaped definition of rhetoric as an art of inquiry does not mean that it is no longer grounded in persuasion. It simply changes persuasion from an end to a necessary means:

> The supreme purpose of persuasion in this view could not be to talk someone else into a preconceived view; rather it must be to engage in mutual inquiry or exploration. In such a world, our rhetorical purpose must always be to perform as well as possible in the same primal symbolic dance which makes us able to dance at all.[16]

Kenneth Burke also locates persuasion within a context of mutual inquiry and knowledge creation. For Burke, symbols in general, and verbal symbols in particular, are in many ways more important than our senses in building our view of reality. In the opening essay of *Language as Symbolic Action*, Burke defines man as "the symbol-using animal":

> Take away our books, and what little do we know about history, biography, even something so "down to earth" as the relative position of seas and continents? What is our "reality" for today (beyond the paper-thin line of our own particular lives) but all this clutter of symbols about the past combined with whatever things we know mainly through maps, magazines, newspapers, and the like about the present?... And however important to us is the tiny sliver of reality each of us has experienced firsthand, the whole overall "picture" is but a construct of our symbol systems.[17]

In the essay "Terministic Screens," also in the *Language as Symbolic Action* volume, Burke expands on the way in which language influences our view of reality. We not only are dependent on symbols for information about events that are physically beyond "the paper-thin line of our own particular lives"; our symbol systems or terministic screens also organize the way we perceive "immediate" reality: "Even if any given terminology is a *reflection* of reality, by its very nature as a terminology it must be a *selection* of reality; and to this extent it must function also as a *deflection* of reality."[18] All our observations, in other words, are profoundly affected by the terminologies in which those observations are made. And because terminologies are communal rather than individual, our reality is made communally: "The human animal, as we know it, *emerges into personality* by first mastering whatever tribal speech happens to be its particular symbolic environment."[19]

For Burke, as for Booth, the knowledge-making properties of language are inextricably connected to its persuasive aspects. As he puts it in *A Rhetoric of Motives*, "The dramatistic view of language, in terms of 'symbolic action,' is exercised about the necessarily *suasive* nature of even the most unemotional scientific nomenclatures."[20] Thus Burke comes, by a somewhat different route, to a view of rhetoric that is in many important respects similar to Booth's. Rhetoric is epistemic—that is, it is part of the process by which we create as well as pass on knowledge.

Burke makes this point especially clear in *The Philosophy of Literary Form*, in which he links drama, dialectic, and rhetoric in his powerful image of the "unending conversation." The image is remarkably parallel to Oakeshott's, except that Burke's rhetorical gaze focuses on the aspect, not of conversation for its own sake, but of debate:

> Imagine that you enter a parlor. You come late. When you arrive, others have long preceded you, and they are engaged in a heated discussion, a discussion too heated for them to pause and tell you exactly what it is about. In fact, the discussion had already begun long before any of them got there, so that no one present is qualified to retrace for you all the steps that had gone before. You listen for a while, until you decide that you have caught the tenor of the argument; then you put in your oar. Someone answers; you answer him; another comes to your defense; another aligns himself against you, to either the embarrassment or gratification of your opponent, depending upon the quality of your ally's assistance. However, the discussion is interminable. The hour grows late, you must depart. And you do depart, with the discussion still vigorously in progress.[21]

Thus for Burke, rhetoric, dialectic, and the drama of human symbolic interaction are inextricably intertwined. Dialectic is simply a particular category of the drama of human symbolic interaction, a brand of interaction "concerned with the maieutic, or midwifery, of philosophic assertion, the ways in which an idea is developed by the 'cooperative competition' of the 'parliamentary.'"[22] The metaphor of dialectic as drama blends easily with a metaphor of dialectic as conversation, for what is drama but conversation placed on a stage for inspection?

This metaphor emphasizes the fact that building each others' minds is a cumulative process that occurs over a vast stretch of time. Each individual act of rhetoric is but one element in a larger conversation, and that conversation is part of a vast discourse which began with the development of symbolization itself. Whatever we collectively and individually know now is the result of an infinitely extended process of sharing and negotiating knowledge, of dialectically testing and improving assertions in all domains of thought.

To refocus attention on the function of rhetoric in this unending human conversation is to effect a major reevaluation of the theoretical boundaries of the discipline, and most particularly of the canon of invention. Invention is traditionally seen as a forward-looking process. The rhetor uses his knowledge of the audience and of the occasion to develop arguments that will be effective when the rhetorical process culminates in the delivery of a speech or the composing of the final draft of a written discourse. The process, in effect, funnels out from the single rhetor toward the audience and moves forward in time from the initial framing of a discourse to its delivery. When rhetoric is situated in an epistemic conversation, however, we can see that it also involves another movement, from the rhetor back into the vast network of conversation that precedes in time that particular exchange. In other words, a full account of rhetoric must recognize that the rhetor is himself an audience. Before he comes to the point of attempting to create belief in others, he has created belief in himself through interaction with countless other selves.

Thus, as Karen Burke LeFevre argues in *Invention as A Social Act*, invention becomes not a private but a public process. It is not just a matter of the rhetor deciding for herself what arguments will persuade an audience, but also a matter of the rhetor developing knowledge in collaboration with countless others. LeFevre draws one of her controlling metaphors from Michel Foucault:

> [Foucault] describes the beginning of a discourse as a re-emergence into an ongoing, never-ending process: "At the moment of speaking, I would like to have perceived a nameless voice, long preceding me, leaving me merely to enmesh myself in it. . . . There would have been no beginnings: instead, speech would proceed from me, while I stood in its path—a slender gap—the point of its possible disappearance." Elaborating on this perspective, one may come to regard discourse not as an isolated event, but rather a constant potentiality that is occasionally evidenced in speech or writing. . . .
>
> Such perspectives suggest that traditional views of an event or act have been misleading when they have presumed that the individual unit—a speech or a written text, an individual hero, a particular battle or discovery—is clearly separable from a larger, continuing

force or stream of events in which it participates. For similar reasons
Jacques Derrida has criticized literary theories that attempt to explain the meaning of a text apart from other texts that precede and
follow it.[23]

This metaphor emphasizes the fact that for modern rhetoricians such as
LeFevre, invention cannot consist, as it did for classical rhetoricians, only
or even primarily of using invention techniques such as topoi to recall
knowledge already stored. Nor can it be limited to the form of invention
that empirical science substitutes for deductive topoi: the direct contemplation of nature by the individual intellect. Rather, it must include
consideration of this "stream of events in which it participates," the
uncountable previous turns of the conversation in which it is embedded
and out of which arises the knowledge that the next rhetorical exchange
will further modify.

This interweaving of the production and consumption of discourse
expands the notion of rhetoric immeasurably. Critics and rhetoricians,
the fences between their territories irrevocably demolished, are increasingly beginning to operate on this expanded definition. In *Protocols of
Reading*, for instance, Robert Scholes acts primarily as a structuralist
literary critic, but firmly situates his criticism in a rhetorical arena:

> What I mean to investigate as rhetoric is the practice of reading, seen
> as an exchange for which textuality is a medium. Under the heading
> of rhetoric, we shall consider reading as a textual economy, in which
> pleasure and power are exchanged between producers and consum-
> ers of texts, always remembering that writers must consume in order
> to produce and that readers must produce in order to consume.[24]

But pointing out that invention *is* a social and a recursive act is only
a starting point. This expansion of the theoretical horizons of rhetoric
requires us to ask a new set of questions about how invention operates.
We must consider not only the role of subject and audience, of topoi, of
rhetorical scene; we must also ask exactly how it is that the rhetor taps the
resources of the unending conversation of which any particular discourse is only a part. In short, how does the rhetor look back before—or
as well as—looking forward? A rhetorical system that does not provide
principles for answering this question is necessarily incomplete, for the
question is entailed by the epistemic perspective to which modern
rhetoric has become committed.

Reading as a Special Form of Invention

Symbolic negotiation of knowledge is not limited to symbols printed on
paper. Symbolicity need not even be verbal. Anything that can be

consciously manipulated by human beings can be read as a symbolic language in which beliefs are formed and shared. Why then do we need a rhetoric specifically of *reading* rather than simply an investigation of the social aspects of invention in general? Why do we need to take the medium into account?

In some ways, of course, we don't. Structuralist inquiries into meaning have gotten on very well by using "reading" as a synecdoche for any form of decoding meaning, treating as "texts" all the productions of humankind from novels to comic books, clothing, and plates of steak and chips. Yet the poststructuralist critique of structuralism is in part based on the claim that moving from one communicative medium to another—from speech to print to architecture to music—changes in nontrivial ways both the problems that must be addressed and the sorts of solutions that can be found.

Print is not just speech written down. It is a medium with its own history, its own constraints, its own psychological peculiarities. In particular, it is a very difficult medium in which to have a conversation. It has become a truism that the reader has no access to the incidental aids that the hearer of speech takes for granted—nuances of voice and facial expression, the ability to ask for clarification, the subtle sources of feedback that allow even large-scale public speaking to be more intimate than the relationship between a reader and a book. But these distancing factors are incidental to the major difference between reading and hearing—the reader's illusion that she is simply absorbing information from a text rather than conversing with, and being persuaded by, another human being.

The particular challenge of a rhetoric of reading is to account for the way in which, despite this illusion of isolation, the reader is actually doing more than absorbing information from disembodied texts. This entails a study of an intricate series of transformations. How does a set of texts that can be held in the hand, texts which proclaim diverse and often contradictory views of the universe, become transformed into a reasonably consistent set of beliefs in the mind of the reader? To put it another way, what are the special characteristics of participating in a "conversation" with others who are absent and in many cases long dead?

To a certain extent, a rhetoric of reading thus conceived is simply a rhetoric of composition considered from another point of view. If a rhetoric of composition is designed to tell a writer how to persuade an audience, it seems simple enough to turn those precepts, by a mere semantic flip, into information for the reader about how writers attempt to persuade her. However, any rhetorical art that goes beyond being a technical manual must be more than a list of means of persuasion. It must be an analysis of the mechanism of persuasion itself and the decisions that go into performing the act. That mechanism and those decisions look very different when we move around the rhetorical triangle to focus on reader rather than writer.

The rhetor's task involves an outward movement; she begins with certain basic propositions that she wants to convey, and then discovers arguments that will support them and a form in which they can be convincingly argued. The discourse thus radiates outward from a more or less unitary center to a more or less diffuse audience, an audience that may consist of hundreds or even millions of individual entities, some not yet born. The rhetor is thus faced with a task of generalization. However well she may know a particular audience, she must be able to use a general knowledge of human nature and of discourse structures in order to predict and to some extent control the responses of that audience.

The reader's task is in certain respects the opposite. The audience is not diffuse, but highly particular—herself. She does not have to ask how to frame propositions that will have the best chance of convincing the largest number of hearers. Rather, she must ask the question that Booth uses as his touchstone in *Modern Dogma*: "When should I change my mind?"[25] This question is synthetic rather than analytic. It does not require the asker to take apart a vast audience and consider what characteristics they may possess as individuals; it requires her to take a disparate group of claims made by individuals, each with his own perspective on the world and his own reasons for seeing it as he does, evaluate them, and actively construct a single view satisfactory to herself. Thus, while a rhetoric of discourse production can tell us some specific reasons why people are persuaded, a rhetoric of discourse consumption must develop an account of how readers sort through the bids made for their assent.

The Shape of a Rhetoric of Reading

In sum, then, a rhetoric of reading will have the following features. In common with any theory of reading, it must be able to account for the first stage of the reading act: the creation of meaning from symbols on paper. However, as a *rhetoric* of reading, it will account for this process in the context of the rhetorical framework. This means that the interaction between reader and text must be seen as being in the service of a larger process: making contact with the mind of another human being.

Moreover, a rhetoric of reading must take into account the place of reading in the epistemic conversation of humankind. This means that it must account not only for the proximate goal of perceiving another person's meanings, but also the ultimate goal of updating a belief system or worldview, a theory about the way the world operates and about the way in which the believer can and should operate within it. To use Booth's terms, such a belief system is a synthesis of "facts" and "values," a set of beliefs about what is and what ought to be. This belief system will in turn contribute to the building of further discourse as the reader takes his turn in the conversation.

This ultimate goal implies a series of intermediate steps. The reader uses texts to supplement the "paper-thin line" of his own experience, to provide additional windows on what is and what ought to be in the world. However, texts refer not just to the world but to a worldview; not to an unmediated state of existence but to the author's perception of the state of things. There are, therefore, two steps between the world and the reader's perception of it: the author's interpretation of the world, and the reader's interpretation of the author's text. The process of reading, then, is not just the interpretation of a text but the interpretation of another person's worldview as presented by a text.

The meaning of a text must not only be interpreted, but evaluated for the power of its persuasive claims; the reader must decide not only what the text says, but if and to what degree what it says is worth believing. As Perelman and Olbrechts-Tyteca note in *The New Rhetoric*, a rhetor does not simply persuade or fail to persuade an audience; rather, "What is characteristic of the adherence of minds is its variable intensity."[26] Seen in the context of reading, this variability of intensity implies that a reader may find different elements of a text persuasive to varying degrees. A rhetoric of reading must answer the question of how readers are induced to assign this variable adherence to the various propositions presented by a text.

Finally, a text never contributes to a belief system in isolation. It will be considered in conjunction with other texts making some similar and some different claims for belief. In some cases the claims will be incompatible, forcing the reader to decide which texts to believe. This is not, however, merely a matter of the reader's picking the text that is the most persuasive and believing it, as if a system of belief were an indivisible unit that can simply be imported from a source and made the reader's. Rather, the reader must synthesize belief from the contributions of the various texts with which she is presented, taking more elements of some and fewer of others. The structure of belief that results from this process will be one in which the elements of the source texts are submerged in new structures that cannot be identified absolutely with any one of the contributing sources.

The challenge of a rhetoric of reading, in short, is to discover the mechanisms of interpretation, evaluation and synthesis by which each individual creates for herself a structure of beliefs that is unique to her, influenced by but not under the control of the texts on which it is erected. That is, a rhetoric of reading will show how reading operates as a major part of rhetorical invention.

An Interdisciplinary Approach to a Rhetoric of Reading

A rhetorical model of reading cannot be generated independently by either a theory of reading or a theory of rhetoric. A theory of rhetoric alone cannot account for the series of acts by which discourse is consumed; a theory of reading alone cannot account for the fact that reading is embedded in a larger process of rhetorical construction of belief. A rhetoric of reading will combine elements of both disciplines in a new synthesis that accounts for a larger process overarching both the production and the consumption of discourse.

The contributions of these two areas of study correspond roughly to the division of the process into the interpretation of texts, and the evaluation and synthesis of the theses offered by them—that is, into the proximate goal of making contact with another mind and the ultimate goal of using that contact to build one's own mind. The process of interpreting sources has traditionally been dealt with by theories of reading rather than by theories of rhetoric. In such theories we would expect to find insights regarding the ways in which readers build a meaning from a text; in particular we would expect to find an explanation of the fact that readers interpret texts differently, remember them differently, and reach different conclusions as to what their authors intended to convey. In short, in theories of reading we would expect to find an answer to the second of the questions posed in the introduction: "How can we describe within a rhetorical framework how meaning is generated during the act of reading? That is, how does a reader know what propositions a writer is trying to persuade her to believe?"

On the other hand, evaluating sources to decide whether they should be included in a system of beliefs is a much more specifically rhetorical problem, for it is a restatement of the question that overarches the entire concept of rhetorical reading: "When should I change my mind?" Thus it is to rhetoric that we should look more directly for the answers to the third and fourth questions implied by a rhetoric of reading: "How does the reader evaluate the propositions presented by individual texts and decide which to be persuaded by?" and "How does the reader negotiate among the claims of various texts in order to develop a unified system of knowledge?"

In short, then, the distinction between the two terms that make up the phrase "rhetoric of reading" can shape the search for insights contributed by reading theory and rhetorical theory. However, it is vital to remember that the two terms are not separate but are two parts of a single concept. Yoking them together has important implications for methodology. In searching for insights through various disciplines that study discourse, we will be looking not just for separate answers to separate questions, but for the materials with which to build a single theory. We must look, then, for what is common, or at least for what is compatible, among the theories. This necessity will act as an important filter. What we take from reading theory will be that which complements and enhances our understanding of reading as a rhetorical process. What we take from rhetorical theory will be that which complements and enhances our understanding of rhetoric as a process whose inventional aspect involves reading.

Although the first stage of the inquiry will emphasize reading theory and the second rhetorical theory, we will be continually shuttling between the two domains, using one as a gloss on the other. The goal is not a theory of reading followed by a theory of rhetoric—we have those already—but an integrated rhetoric of reading that subsumes both into a single account that, despite my divisions of convenience, describes a single process: rhetorical reading.

Notes

1. Aristotle, *Rhetoric*, trans. Lane Cooper (Englewood Cliffs: Prentice-Hall, 1932), 7.

2. George A. Kennedy, *Classical Rhetoric and Its Christian and Secular Tradition from Ancient to Modern Times* (Chapel Hill: University of North Carolina Press, 1980), 4.

3. Donald C. Bryant, *Rhetorical Dimensions in Criticism* (Baton Rouge: Louisiana State University Press, 1973), 14.

4. Plato, *Gorgias*, trans. W. C. Helmbold (Indianapolis: Bobbs-Merrill, 1952), 27.

5. Plato, *Phaedrus*, trans. W. C. Helmbold and W. G. Rabinowitz (Indianapolis: Bobbs-Merrill, 1956), 72.

6. Lloyd Bitzer, "The Rhetorical Situation," in *Contemporary Theories of Rhetoric: Selected Readings*, ed. Richard L. Johannesen (New York: Harper, 1971), 386.

7. Kenneth Burke, *Language as Symbolic Action* (Berkeley: University of California Press, 1966), 46.

8. Thomas S. Kuhn, *The Structure of Scientific Revolutions*, 2nd ed. (Chicago: University of Chicago Press, 1970).

9. Michael Polanyi, *Personal Knowledge: Towards a Post-Critical Philosophy* (Chicago: University of Chicago Press, 1958), 150.

10. Michael Oakeshott, "The Voice of Poetry in the Conversation of Mankind," in *Rationalism in Politics and Other Essays* (London: Methuen, 1962), 199.

11. Wayne C. Booth, *Modern Dogma and the Rhetoric of Assent* (Chicago: University of Chicago Press, 1974), 101.

12. Booth, 105.

13. Booth, 108–09.

14. Booth, 126.

15. Booth, 11.

16. Booth, 127.

17. Burke, 5.

18. Burke, 45.

19. Burke, 53.

20. Kenneth Burke, *A Rhetoric of Motives* (Berkeley: University of California Press, 1950), 45.

21. Kenneth Burke, *The Philosophy of Literary Form: Studies in Symbolic Action* (Berkeley: University of California Press, 1941), 110–11.

22. Burke, *The Philosophy of Literary Form*, 107.

23. Karen Burke LeFevre, *Invention as a Social Act* (Carbondale: Southern Illinois University Press, 1987), 41–42.

24. Robert Scholes, *Protocols of Reading* (New York: Yale University Press, 1989), 90.

25. Booth, 12.

26. Chaim Perelman and L. Olbrechts-Tyteca, *The New Rhetoric: A Treatise on Argumentation*, trans. John Wilkinson and Purcell Weaver (Notre Dame: University of Notre Dame Press, 1969), 4.

2 Reading as Construction;
Reading as Communication

Why Does Rhetoric Need
a Theory of Interpretation?

The rhetorical view of reading insists that our "selves," the bundles of beliefs and values that give each of us our unique identities, are created through rhetoric. Written texts are an important component of the rhetorical input that has formed us, and a particularly important part of the rhetorical input that has formed our more abstract and intellectual ideas—that part of our personality concerned with what is beyond the "paper-thin line of our own particular lives," as Burke puts it.

The way we believe or disbelieve certain texts clearly varies from one individual to the next. If you present a text that is remotely controversial to a group of people, some will be convinced by it and some not, and those who are convinced will be convinced in different degrees. The task of a rhetoric of reading is to explain systematically how these differences arise—how people are persuaded differently by texts. We could assume that all readers of a given text see essentially the same things but evaluate them differently and base different conclusions on them. This is certainly an intuitively reasonable explanation of how readers reach different conclusions from their reading. A theory of reading that focused purely on this aspect of reading would be purely a theory of judgment, and would not have to address the problem of interpretation at all. However, to discuss judgment without discussing interpretation is to imply that reading is an algorithmic process that all competent readers will perform in the same way. But the domain of rhetoric is not the domain of the exact and the algorithmic, of propositions about which a disagreement is a sign of error. It is the domain of the contingent, of propositions that, in Aristotle's words, "appear to admit of two possibilities," for "on matters which admit of no alternative, which necessarily were, or will be, or are, certainties, no one deliberates."[1] The more we can characterize interpretation as a contingent process, the more we can build a model of reading interpenetrated at all points by the rhetorical viewpoint. Therefore, before we can ask how different readers are persuaded to adopt different views by the texts they read, we must first ask the second of the questions listed in the preface: "How does a reader know what propositions a writer is trying to persuade her to believe?"

In addition, rhetorical theory must incorporate a theory of interpretation because of the increasing closeness of rhetorical and literary theory. In chapter 1, I pointed out that any rhetorical theory must assume that the recipient's response is at least partly predictable. This assumption, however, has usually been treated simply *as* an assumption, an article of faith. The idea that it could be otherwise never occurred to the ancient rhetoricians. The idea occurs to Wayne Booth, for he devotes quite a bit of space in *Modern Dogma* to insisting that meaning is shareable:

> Not only do we talk and write and create art and mathematical symbols and act as if we shared them: we really do share them, sometimes. Sometimes we *understand* each other. . . . In short, we know other minds, sometimes, to some degree. That we often do not, and that the knowledge is never complete, is at this point irrelevant, though it has sometimes been talked about as though we were hopelessly alone.[2]

Booth never tells us who it is that talks about understanding this way, but it is not hard to guess who he wants us to think of: Bleich, Fish, Derrida, de Man, and all the other literary critics who solve the problem of unstable interpretation by denying that texts have any stable meaning, or that it matters.

I will say more about these critical theories, especially those of Bleich and Fish, in the next section of this chapter. For the time being, suffice it to say that they argue in a variety of ways for a view of language that, if sincerely held, would make rhetoric impossible by denying its most fundamental postulate: that we can deliberately and predictably influence each other through language. Booth is certainly right to argue that we simply know, without needing proof, that it can't be so. We could not get on with our lives if it were so.

But for rhetorical theory, as opposed to daily practice, this common-sense assertion of faith finally will not do. The relationship between rhetoric and literature is too close for us simply to wave away theories of indeterminacy. In fact it is now closer than it has ever been. In *A Speech-Act Theory of Literature*, for instance, Mary Louise Pratt argues that neither formal features of texts nor the presence or absence of fictivity can distinguish literature from non-literature.[3] The same sorts of tropes that are sometimes held to characterize poetic language can be shown to crowd into "non-poetic" or "ordinary" language. Likewise, "ordinary language" is replete with fictive speech acts such as imitation, joking, hyperbole, hypotheses, and even extended narrative. Such counterexamples argue that if there is a distinction to be made between literature and non-literature, we cannot find it in the text.

Louise Rosenblatt makes the same case in *The Reader, The Text, The Poem*. Rosenblatt claims that what we feel intuitively to be "literature" cannot be distinguished from non-literature on the basis of the text itself. What is different is the *use* that we make of a text. Any text may be read in either an "aesthetic" or an "efferent" mode (or in some combination of the two). Efferent reading is reading "in which the primary concern of the reader is with what he will carry away from the reading"; aesthetic reading is reading in which "the reader's attention is centered directly on what he is living through during his relationship with that particular text."[4] The difference between literature and non-literature is therefore centered in the reader, in a "shift of attention" that divides literary from non-literary reading.

In practical terms, of course, there are types of texts, such as works conventionally labeled as novels, plays, and poems, which most frequently trigger aesthetic reading acts, and others (Rosenblatt's paradigmatic case is the instructions on a fire extinguisher) which are almost always read efferently. But the point is that if there is no way of reliably distinguishing literary from non-literary texts, and if many voices in modern literary theory argue that literary texts have no stable meaning, then we cannot simply *assume* that rhetorical texts have stable meaning, for there is no way to establish what is a "rhetorical" text as opposed to a literary one. We need more than an *assertion that* we can really know something about what others are saying to us; we need a *model of how* we know.

However, because rhetoric has tended to treat the link between rhetor and audience as an unacknowledged assumption, it will be difficult to build a model of interpretation from within rhetoric. On the other hand, literary theory has a long history of dealing with multiple interpretations, for it has had to take account of the fact that literary works typically give rise to interpretations so different from one another that it sometimes seems as if readers have read different texts. Attempts to put interpretation on a more "scientific" footing by defining more exactly the critical task and by attempting to document in detail the effects of various literary devices have only compounded the problem. One has only to review the incredible variety of interpretations produced by members of the New Critical movement to realize how impossible it is to devise a single consistent meaning for any literary work.[5] As a result, literary theory has tended to be highly tolerant of multiple interpretation and to seek explanations for it instead of trying to eliminate it. It is to literary theory, then, that I will look for one important ingredient of a rhetoric of reading: highly developed theories of how meaning is constructed and how it varies systematically from reader to reader.

Of the wide range of literary theories available, the category that bears most closely on this inquiry is "reader-response" or "audience-oriented" theories such as those of Stanley Fish, Louise Rosenblatt, and Wolfgang Iser. I single out this group of critics because they are particularly interested in a question central to the present inquiry: what does the reader bring to the transaction between rhetor and audience?

Literary theories of reading, however, are not the only fertile source of insight for a theory of rhetorical reading. Even if we cannot reliably distinguish between literary and non-literary *texts*, it is clear that there are different types of reading *acts*, and it is, in fact, what Rosenblatt calls the "efferent" reading act that rhetoric is most concerned with. The rhetorical reader is reading primarily, not just incidentally, for the purpose of updating a system of beliefs, and will typically (though not exclusively) be doing so by reading the sorts of texts that are conventionally labeled "non-literature": newspaper accounts, polemics, research articles, books of history and science.

Although it may be possible to extend literary theory to cover such types of reading—indeed, I will be doing so many times in this chapter—it would be foolish to limit this inquiry to such theories when other reading theories more obviously concerned with efferent reading lie ready to hand. I am referring to discourse-processing theories of comprehension. These theories span a number of disciplines such as linguistics, education, developmental psycho-social linguistics, cognitive psychology, and cognitive science.[6] The common ground in these theories is that they are not centrally theories of language, of code systems, or of texts. Rather, they are theories of mental processes. They use empirical data to create models of the ways in which the human mind generates and represents meaning when confronted with symbol systems such as written texts. These theories are sometimes applied to literary texts, but often are not concerned with specific types of texts; indeed, they are often not concerned with texts as such at all, but with processes that operate at the level of the single sentence. Their chief concern is not textual but cognitive; they seek an understanding primarily of the mind as a language processing instrument, rather than of the language that is processed.

Rand J. Spiro characterizes the goal of reading as seen from the discourse-processing point of view:

> When you are reading the latest installment of *Newsweek* about the energy crisis, if you have been following it in the past you will probably not endeavor to form a complete insular representation of the article as your goal of understanding. Rather, your goal will probably be to integrate what you are reading with what you already know of the subject, with special attention to information that is new. That is, your goal of reading is to *update* your knowledge.[7]

This process—that is, seeking out the new information in texts and amalgamating it with a preexisting mental structure—is precisely the sort of reading act that a rhetoric of reading is designed to account for. Nor is such updating of knowledge seen simply as a matter of accumulating factual knowledge. As Schank and Abelson put it,

> Lurking beneath the surface [of discourse-processing theories] is an interest in the ingredients of personal belief systems about the world, which dispose people toward alternative social, religious, or political actions.[8]

Processing discourse can thus be seen as a matter of accumulating and organizing knowledge as a basis for action, a matter clearly within the realm of rhetoric. Discourse-processing theories of comprehension, then, can offer a useful foil for literary theories of meaning because they focus on the efferent reading act, which is clearly rhetorical, rather than on the aesthetic reading act, about which many arhetorical theories of meaning have been proposed.

The main contribution of rhetorical theory to this stage of the account is to suggest the parameters of the investigation. According to rhetorical theory, there are four main variables in any rhetorical interaction: the classic rhetorical triangle of the writer, the text, and the reader, plus the external context or rhetorical situation in which the act is situated. Seen as a rhetorical act, reading must always be situated as part of a larger process in which these four elements co-operate to generate meaning. Only in such co-operation, in which meaning is both generated and constrained by this complex four-way transaction, can meaning be constituted as a rhetorical act.

Reading as a Constructive Act

To begin constructing a model of rhetorical reading, let us expand on the point made briefly in the previous section: meaning does not reside exclusively in the text. This claim is made vehemently by both reader-response criticism and by cognitive science. In fact, this argument is so deeply entrenched in both bodies of theory that it seems almost fatuous to argue that reading is not passive. However, it will be useful to survey these theories to provide a sense of the extent to which they view reading as constructive, and of the various kinds of constructive processes that have been proposed.

In *Is There a Text In This Class?* Stanley Fish argues that reading is not so much a matter of discerning what is there as it is a matter of "knowing how to *produce* what can thereafter be said to be there. Interpretation is not the art of construing but the art of constructing. Interpreters do not decode poems; they make them."[9] He illustrates this point with an anecdote. One day, when a class in metaphysical poetry entered his classroom, the following reading list was on the board:

> Jacobs-Rosenbaum
> Levin
> Thorne
> Hayes
> Ohman (?)

He told the class that it was a seventeenth-century poem, and the students proceeded to produce a meaning commensurate with their understanding of seventeenth-century poetry, complete with metaphysical conceits and rich religious significance. Fish rejects the possible argument that the "poem" reading was simply an interpretation forced on a text that contained the "natural" meaning of an assignment:

> An assignment no more compels its own recognition than does a poem; rather, as in the case of a poem, the shape of an assignment emerges when someone looks at something identified as one with assignment-seeing eyes, that is, with eyes which are capable of seeing the words as already embedded within the institutional structure that makes it possible for assignments to have a sense. The ability to see, and therefore to make, an assignment is no less a learned ability than the ability to see, and therefore to make, a poem. Both are constructed artifacts, the products and not the producers of interpretation.[10]

This particular example seems somewhat contrived. It seems likely that Fish's students were putting him on, or he us; as Robert Scholes trenchantly puts it, "If you play cards with Stanley Fish, don't let him bring his own deck."[11] But Fish's basic point is well taken, and finds wide support among reader-response critics: the reader, these critics agree, is an active creator rather than a passive recipient of meaning. Louise Rosenblatt, for instance, will not go as far as Fish does in assigning autonomy to the reader (I will discuss this point more thoroughly later in this chapter); however, she insists that the text is only one of the elements of the reading process. The other is the reader, who actively organizes out of the inert materials of the text a personally constructed, personally experienced "poem" that she describes as an "event in time":

> It is not an object or an ideal entity. It happens during a coming-together, a compenetration, of a reader and a text. The reader brings to the text his past experience and present personality. Under the magnetism of the ordered symbols of the text, he marshals his resources and crystallizes out from the stuff of memory, thought, and feeling a new order, a new experience, which he sees as the poem.[12]

This "poem," as opposed to the black marks on paper that constitute the "text," is variable. It is an event created by "a specific reader and a specific text at a specific time and place: change any of these, and there occurs a different circuit, a different event—a different poem."[13] Her term for the creation of this event is "evoking" the poem.

To describe the interaction of text and reader, Rosenblatt borrows from Dewey and Bentley the term "transaction," which she describes as "an ongoing process in which the elements or factors are, one might say, aspects of a total situation, each conditioned by and conditioning the other."[14] She finds this term particularly useful because unlike other terms such as "interpretation," which suggests that the reader acts on the text, or "response," which suggests that the text acts on the reader, "transaction" implies no directionality. Rather, it suggests a more or less equal contribution by both parties. It is this suggestion of balanced contribution, a balance that is essential to the rhetorical view of language, that makes Rosenblatt's concept of the "transaction" especially useful to a rhetorical view of reading.

This concept of an abstract entity produced by the interaction of text and reader is repeated in the work of other reader-response critics. In *The Act of Reading*, Wolfgang Iser also argues that the work of art does not have a single "meaning" that can be extracted from it. For Iser, texts initiate "performances" of meaning, creating a "virtual work" that, like Rosenblatt's "poem," is not identical either with the text or with the reader:

> [It] must be situated somewhere between the two. It must inevitably be virtual in character, as it cannot be reduced to the reality of the text or to the subjectivity of the reader, and it is from this virtuality that it derives its dynamism.[15]

This concept of an actively constructed "virtual work" is not limited to literary theory; it also appears in cognitive theories of the comprehension process. Until fairly recently, discourse-processing theories have been dominated by the assumption described by Goetz and Armbruster as "the implicit assumption that text structure and content are inherent in the text."[16] However, this position is rapidly shifting, and many recent studies are taking a constructive approach similar in many respects to that taken by reader-response criticism.

Frank Smith's 1971 work *Understanding Reading* broke ground in this area.[17] Smith opposed the prevailing assumption that readers first decode a text into sounds on a character-by-character basis, assemble those sounds into words, and then comprehend text as a linear sequence of words thus decoded. If reading proceeded in such a step-by-step fashion, Smith argues, the eye and brain simply could not process the incredible amount of raw information involved. In order to read efficiently, readers rely instead on nonvisual information such as their knowledge of language and of the world to predict what the next few letters, words, or phrases will probably be. They check these predictions not by attending to all the visual features of the text but merely by sampling it to confirm or deconfirm the predicted meaning. Thus practiced readers can comprehend far more text in a given space of time than they would be able to if they were processing discrete units of data and then assembling a meaning.

Since 1971, discourse-processing theories have been attempting to account for meaning construction at an ever more global level. Particularly interesting results have been obtained by using texts that have been deliberately salted with ambiguities. These texts, although read efferently rather than aesthetically, produce variant readings similar to those that literary theories have tried to account for. In a seminal study entitled "Frameworks for Comprehending Discourse," Richard C. Anderson et al. report a study using the following text:

> Every Saturday night, four good friends got together. When Jerry, Mike, and Pat arrived, Karen was sitting in her living room writing some notes. She quickly gathered the cards and stood up to greet her friends at the door. They followed her into the living room but as usual they couldn't agree on exactly what to play. Jerry eventually took a stand and set things up. Finally, they began to play. Karen's recorder filled the room with soft and pleasant music. Early in the evening, Mike noticed Pat's hand and the many diamonds. As the night progressed the tempo of play increased. Finally, a lull in the activities occurred. Taking advantage of this, Jerry pondered the arrangement in front of him. Mike interrupted Jerry's reverie and said, "Let's hear the score." They listened carefully and commented on their performance. When the comments were all heard, exhausted but happy, Karen's friends went home.[18]

This text has two fairly obvious interpretations: a night of playing cards or a night of playing music. Subjects who were already interested in games (such as physical education majors) tended to see the first interpretation more often, while subjects who were already interested in music (such as music majors), tended to see the second. These results did not surprise the researchers, and they certainly would not have surprised Stanley Fish. But these two obvious interpretations did not exhaust the possibilities; in fact, subjects reported a wide variety of interpretations, none of which was in obvious conflict with the text. Interpreting this study in a later paper, Carey and Harste describe the reading process using a transactional terminology explicitly borrowed from Rosenblatt:

> These findings were consistent with the notion of the reading process
> as semantic transaction. This conceptualization provides for reading
> as a dynamic and vital process that denies the supremacy of the
> author while anticipating shades of subtlety among the interpreta-
> tions made by readers. In this view, comprehension is much less
> monolithic than conventional wisdom might suggest. Thus . . . each
> reading act constitutes a unique transactional event.[19]

Rand Spiro goes even further. Arguing from similar ambiguous
passages, Spiro concludes that language does not create meaning:

> What language provides is a skeleton, a blueprint for the creation of
> meaning. Such skeletal representations must then be enriched and
> embellished so that they conform with the understander's preexist-
> ing world views and the operative purposes of understanding at a
> given time.[20]

What reader-response critics say about the aesthetic reading act, then,
is strongly echoed in what cognitive theorists say about the efferent
reading act. When readers come to such different conclusions about
what they read that they seem to have read different texts, there is a sense
in which this is true: they have looked at the same characters on paper,
but have seen quite different meanings. To combine terms from Rosenblatt
and Iser, they have read the same texts but evoked different virtual
works.

Materials of Construction: The Repertoire

To conclude that meaning *is constructed* is not by itself very interesting;
we also need to be able to explain *how* writer, text, reader, and situation
cooperate rhetorically to produce meaning. We can subdivide this
question into three parts. First, if the reader contributes to the evocation
of the virtual work, what specific materials does she bring to its construction and how are they organized? Second, how can we account for the
fact that not only do different readers evoke different works, but the
same reader will evoke different works on different occasions? Finally,
and most important for a rhetorical view of reading, what are the
constraints on interpretation that allow for rhetorical interchange?
    In answer to the first question, Rosenblatt claims that although the
general meanings of words are reasonably stable and common to all
speakers of the language, these shared "dictionary" meanings form only
the basic substratum of meaning on which the reader erects her more
personal construction. The reader will bring to the words of the text a
wealth of personal associations drawn from an interplay of shared social
and uniquely personal experience. She will have learned the denotational

meaning of a word in specific contexts, both verbal and physical, that give it associations unlike those of any other reader. It is these associations with the author's words, not the dead words on the page themselves, that provide the materials out of which the reader weaves the virtual work, her own personal and transient image of the text and the meanings that it presents.

Stanley Fish, while never denying that the reader's response to a text is profoundly affected by the personal associations he attaches to words, strikes a different balance between the personal and the social. His most original and important claim is that interpretations are made, not just by the reader as an individual, nor even by the reader in cooperation with the text and the writer, but by the reader in cooperation with the institutions in which she is embedded. The meanings we make from any symbol system, whether written prose, poetry, gesture, abstract art, or computer programming language, are regulated by communally constructed and communally negotiated rules of interpretation. The rules that Fish's students followed in building a seventeenth-century poem from a list of names were those created collectively by seventeenth-century poets and their audiences, reinterpreted through two centuries of poetic composition and criticism, handed on to students through university English classes, and finally activated by their belief that the list of names on the blackboard was a poem. The alternate construction of those characters, as a reading assignment rather than a poem, was guided by an alternate set of rules, less formally passed on but equally formed by communal expectations, that govern what an assignment is, what a list is, etc. These sorts of rules, by which any set of symbols is given meaning and without which no set of symbols can have meaning, define various overlapping *interpretive communities* that are constituted by interpretive rules shared by those who belong to them.

Fish does not suggest that these rules are fixed. On the contrary, he claims that they are in continual flux, and that one of the major functions of the critical enterprise is to renegotiate the rules of interpretation. The interpretive communities set limits on interpretation, but there are no theoretical limits on the possible shape that interpretive communities can take. Interpretive strategies that might strike us as nonsense (such as Fish's own example of Blake's "The Tyger" interpreted as an allegory of the digestive tract) strike us as nonsense only because we do not belong to an interpretive community that can legitimize such an interpretation. Such a community could grow up at any time, impelled either by external or internal forces: it may be discovered that Blake had a preoccupation with the digestive system, or it may happen that interpreters begin moving spontaneously in the direction of such a set of interpretive conventions in sufficiently large numbers that they can begin to constitute their own interpretive community and perhaps persuade others to join.

There are a number of difficulties with Fish's approach to meaning. Fish does not provide a very satisfactory explanation, for instance, of how the members of a given interpretive community could begin to persuade others to join them, given that their interpretations and their entire mode of discourse would, by his own definition, be unintelligible to those outside the community. Nonetheless, the concept of interpretive communities is a useful one. It explains not only differences in interpretation but also similarities, accounting for the ways in which interpretations, though always differing from one interpreter to the next, tend to cluster in groups and even form formal schools of interpretation. Most importantly, it explains the influence of communal warrants of interpretation not just in terms of shared denotative meanings of words but also in terms of shared larger structures. Such structures allow social forces greater control over the way interpretations are made.

Iser provides yet another perspective on the ways in which the materials of interpretation are organized, a perspective that represents yet another way of mixing the private and the public aspects of interpretation. Although Iser argues that the meaning of a text is evoked by the reader, this "is not the same as saying that comprehension is arbitrary, for the mixture of determinacy and indeterminacy conditions the interaction between text and reader."[21] One of the most important sources of determinacy in this mixture, the prime ingredient in the instructions for the building of the situation, is what Iser calls the "repertoire":

> The repertoire consists of all the familiar territory within the text. This may be in the form of references to earlier works, or to social and historical norms, or to the whole culture from which the text has emerged.[22]

This repertoire affects the evocation of the virtual work by forming "schemata," that is, preexisting patterns which condition the way meaning is formed out of the individual experience of the reader. Iser borrows this concept from gestalt psychology by way of Gombrich's theory of art, which holds that the artist uses schemata to organize the chaotic materials of perception and so reduce the contingency of the world into a coherent set of expectations.

For Iser, these schemata are present in the text:

> The text mobilizes the subjective knowledge present in all kinds of readers and directs it to one particular end. However varied this knowledge may be, the reader's subjective contribution is controlled by the given framework. It is as if the schema were a hollow form into which the reader is invited to pour his own store of knowledge.[23]

Other critical writers, including ones who have been heavily influenced by cognitive science such as McCormick and Waller, share this sense that the text somehow "contains" a repertoire of values and conventions that act on the reader.[24]

In some ways this seems extremely odd in view of what we know of the constructive nature of the reading act. Texts are nothing but black marks on paper. They cannot act, and anything they "do" is actually being done by the reader. Kantz declares quite firmly,

> I suspect that Iser and other critics frequently discuss as text features concepts that are probably reified as sets of reader activities, because they have an impoverished model of the reading processes, especially the lower-level processes. This impoverished model causes them to undervalue the work done by the reader in representing the text.[25]

Yet in another sense this reification is justified as it reflects an important aspect of certain types of schemata. When schemata are widely shared, they do indeed become a hollow form into which the reader's personal store of knowledge is poured. They act as a structure of constraints, giving public form to the reader's private associations. Just as we perceive our visual experience of objects as being "out there" in the world rather than in our brains and retinas, so readers perceive shared schemata as being "out there" in the text. They are actually "in" the transaction between text and reader, where powerful social forces guide the individual act of evoking a virtual work, yet they are perceived as being in the text because their shareability means that the words of the text tend to trigger at least roughly similar reactions from a large number of people.

The repertoire is in some ways more general and less flexible than Fish's interpretive structures; it is a structure of general knowledge that informs the interpretive process rather than a set of specific rules as to how interpretation is to proceed. It is therefore a much larger and more generally available set of materials, and much less prone to variation. Knowledge can be added to and modified, but not rewritten in the way that a set of rules can. Still, the repertoire functions in much the same way as an interpretive community. By providing a hollow form into which the reader's personal store of knowledge is poured, the schemata formed by the repertoire act as a structure of constraints, giving public form to the reader's private associations and accounting for the influence of social forces on the individual interpretive act.

These insights from literary criticism are very closely paralleled by discourse-processing models of comprehension, in which the term "schema" is widely used to designate a concept very similar to Iser's.

Schemata are structures that organize the reader's knowledge so as to make it accessible when needed. Researchers do not agree on exactly what schemata are, how they function, or even whether they are best described as structures or processes. But there is general agreement as to what they do and what phenomena they are able to explain.[26]

Schemata are used, as David Rumelhart puts it, to explain how the mind functions in "interpreting sensory data (both linguistic and non-linguistic), in retrieving information from memory, in organizing actions, in determining goals and subgoals, in allocating resources, and, generally, in guiding the flow of processing in the system"—in short, in managing knowledge.[27] Rumelhart describes a schema as a means of packaging knowledge in memory so that it is not just raw data but an organized set of information. It is derived from personal experience, but is highly abstracted into a general model; we have schemata for playing music, getting together with friends, shopping, going to a restaurant, and so on. "It is useful," explains Rumelhart, "to think of a schema as a kind of informal, private, unarticulated theory about the nature of the events, objects, or situations that we face. The total set of schemata we have available for interpreting our world in a sense constitutes our private theory of the nature of reality."[28]

The chief purpose of these sets of information is to help us interpret and assimilate new knowledge. It is by fitting a text to known schemata that a reader is able to understand it. Readers processing Anderson's card-game/music-night text, for instance, seek to comprehend the ambiguous terms of the text by searching for a schema into which all of the elements can be incorporated in a coherent plot. As I mentioned earlier, readers who are most familiar with music will tend to select a music-oriented schema, triggered by words such as "notes," "play," and especially "music." Once they have selected this schema, they will understand the rest of the text in accordance with their experience of what it means to enjoy a night of playing music together with friends. The other ambiguous terms will be interpreted in light of this schema. Readers more familiar with games are more likely to build a stable virtual work according to that schema.

Schemata do not force a particular interpretation. Rather, they are tentative estimates of significance, tried on for size and then abandoned in favor of a better whenever necessary. If terms occur in the text which cannot be interpreted in accordance with the first schema selected, the schema will be abandoned and another tried. This change of schema will not only affect the construal of subsequent text but will force a reevaluation of text already read. The entire virtual work, to use Iser's term, is highly plastic and shifts in accordance with the schema that the reader is attempting to apply at a given moment.

We are all familiar with this process from our own experience of reading. We build an estimate of an author's meaning, but continually revise it as we encounter new information. Only occasionally does this experience come to consciousness, as when we read a passage that suddenly forces us to revise our entire estimate of meaning. This gives us the familiar experience of saying suddenly, "Aha, so *that's* what she meant all along." Researchers make the experience obvious by using deliberately ambiguated texts such as Anderson's card-game/music-night text. But all discourse is inherently ambiguous, and as the questions asked about a text become more complex—as we move from trying to decide between a music night and a game of cards to trying to decide whether Kant thinks that all experience is imaginary or not—the ambiguity of language rises dramatically. The schema provides a way of resolving that ambiguity and constructing a meaningful work.

Literary theory and discourse-processing theory, then, agree that what the reader brings to the work, what makes interpretation possible, is the familiar: the conventions of discourse, the world knowledge, the linguistic knowledge, the personal associations, that allow him to evoke a meaning from lifeless text. While the text in the hands of this or that reader will always contain the same characters in the same order—the same "visual information," to use Smith's terminology—each reader will bring to it a different repertoire of nonvisual information—that is, a different set of interpretive conventions, linguistic and world knowledge, and personal associations organized as schemata. Expanding Iser's terminology, we can call this entire set of elements that the reader brings to the reading act the reader's "repertoire." This repertoire, which will inevitably vary from one reader to the next, provides one component of a theory of rhetorical interpretation.

Materials of Construction: The Rhetorical Situation

Differences in repertoire from one reader to the next can explain why one reader may interpret a text differently from another. However, readings can also vary from transaction to transaction, even when successive transactions involve the same reader. Such variations occur not only in literary reading, in which one may completely reverse one's appraisal of a work upon rereading; they also happen in efferent reading. One may, for instance, come back to a book or article read months or even days before and see quite different things in it. Complete reappraisals of a text—evocations of different virtual works—can even occur between one act of thinking about a text and another, without a physical rereading. These are different from the changes I referred to earlier, in which a new passage of text suddenly shows a tentative schema to be inadequate and forces the reader to select a new one. Here I am referring to changes in interpretation that occur *after* at least one complete pass through the text.

These variations could, of course, simply result from performance errors. Certainly, readers will miss some important aspects of a text on a first reading and must rectify these errors on subsequent readings. However, to base an explanation of interpretive variation entirely on random error, on cognitive failure, would eat away at the assumption of predictability upon which a rhetorical system is founded. This would make the model less useful as a means of illuminating the way knowledge is built through rhetorical interchange, for it could not describe as completely how belief systems are linked to the texts which inform them.

However, the model as developed thus far cannot provide a more principled account of such variations. The reader's repertoire could be expected to change only slowly as new information gradually forms new schemata and modifies old ones.[29] Because of this relative stability over time, changes in the reader's store of knowledge cannot entirely account for changes in interpretation that may be both sweeping and sudden. In order to account for these variations in a principled way, a rhetorical model of reading must have additional ways of accounting for variant interpretation.

Iser's concept of the "wandering viewpoint" is a useful element in such a model of interpretation. For Iser, the reader can only see the work from a certain perspective at any given time. He uses the term "theme" to refer to the view of the work with which the reader is involved at a given moment; the other potential viewpoints, which continue to affect the reader but are not currently focal, constitute the "horizon." The perspectives by means of which the reader views the theme are supplied by this horizon, the traces of all the previous themes with which the reader has been involved. But the reader cannot stand still in contemplation of a single theme. As her viewpoint moves through the text, the present theme must become horizon as another theme becomes focal. Thus reading is a dynamic act of constantly shifting perspectives. These perspectives evoke a virtual work that does not have a single shape but constantly changes as the moving viewpoint brings into focal attention different themes viewed from the vantage point of different horizons.

Discourse-processing theory supplies an alternative metaphor to describe an essentially similar process. In "Text, Attention, and Memory in Reading Research," Robert De Beaugrande explains shifting representations of text in terms of the physical limitations of the reader's working memory. He defines this working memory as "a store that (in contrast to short- or long-term memory) can be defined not by range, but by its actions; working memory addresses ongoing input that demands processing in order to constitute comprehension."[30] The working memory can hold a representation of only a small portion of the text at any one time. To allow the reader access to the entire text, the information from this working store must be added to a larger mental representation (called by De Beaugrande a "text-world model") that is available for consultation but which is being constantly updated from the "ongoing input." This internal representation consists not just of text passed into memory in raw form but of *interpreted* text; it is the reader's estimate of what the text means, not of its surface features. In this respect it is a close analog of Iser's "virtual work," and like that virtual work it is not static but an event, constantly shifting as the reader's attention—the "wandering viewpoint"—addresses first one text segment and then another.

Here we have an additional element of variation that can explain differences between one reading and another. As Iser points out, the reader's wandering viewpoint will never wander the same way through the same work twice. Even if, as Iser argues, the goal of efferent reading is to reduce uncertainty and evoke a stable meaning from the text,[31] this goal can never be completely fulfilled. As each new theme comes into view, the new perspectives provided by old themes (now become horizons) will demand that it be read in a more or less different way. "What has been read," claims Iser, "shrinks in the memory to a foreshortened background, but it is being constantly evoked in a new context and so modified by new correlates that instigate a restructuring of past syntheses."[32] This is not simply to say that a reader will read the text in a different order each time. It is to say that, even if the reader's eyes take the same linear path through the book, her attention—the wandering viewpoint—will be different because each experience of reading will have been modified by the previous one.

Iser's use of the term "wandering" might seem to suggest that the movement of the viewpoint is more or less undirected. The text, one is tempted to think, establishes a landscape and leaves the reader's viewpoint to find its own way through it. However, Iser sees the viewpoint as being directed by a special feature of literary texts: textual "blanks," indeterminate areas in the texts that can only be filled with the reader's projections of meaning. These blanks break up the process of evoking a coherent, unified virtual work, forcing an alternation of theme and horizon and impelling the reader toward "ideation." According to Iser, this "ideation" is maximized in literary texts that are maximally impeded, forcing the reader to engage in maximal ideation in order to construct the work. In short, in Iser's formulation the literary work is rich, vivid, and effective in proportion to the degree to which the wandering viewpoint is forced by blanks into ever-new constructive activity.

In a literary theory of reading, a high degree of uncertainty can be seen not as a drawback but as a virtue. If the paramount purpose of a reading act is aesthetic experience, it is not primarily important that the reader be lead to a specific form of ideation to fulfill specific persuasive goals. The shift in perspectives provoked by the text can be a sufficient goal in itself. In a rhetoric of reading, however, we cannot leave the model here, for a rhetorical theory demands not just ideation, but ideation that is controlled in principled ways. To work toward a more rhetorical account of the wandering viewpoint, we must reformulate the concept in rhetorical rather than literary terms so that, while preserving Iser's valuable insight, we can ask more rhetorical questions of it.

In *The New Rhetoric*, Perelman and Olbrechts-Tyteca develop the concept of "presence." Presence is a principle of variability that in some ways parallels Iser's wandering viewpoint from a rhetorical point of view. Perelman and Olbrechts-Tyteca define presence as a variable in persuasion that acts in concert with the selection of arguments. It is not enough, they warn, for the rhetor to select the data and the arguments that he feels will be persuasive to the audience. Those elements must be made *present* to the audience; the audience must be made to pay attention to them, to feel them as immediate, and thereby to be affected by them. The challenge of the rhetor is "to make present, by verbal magic alone, what is actually absent but what he considers important to his argument, or, by making them more present, to enhance the value of some of the elements of which one has actually been made conscious."[33]

This concept can enrich Iser's conception of the wandering viewpoint. We can see the text as a landscape through which the reader's viewpoint wanders, but that landscape is not fixed. It varies according to the degree of presence with which each of its features is endowed. The elements of the text that are endowed with the most presence for a particular reader at a particular time are those to which he will naturally pay the greatest attention. It is to those that his wandering viewpoint will return most frequently in order to contemplate their significance.

This perspective suggests that the question about what guides the wandering viewpoint should be rephrased as a question about what endows certain elements of the text with more or less presence. Part of the answer, of course, must surely be the rhetorical techniques used by the writer: the selection of arguments, arrangement, and style that he uses to make his discourse maximally effective. These are means by which the writer controls effect by controlling the text. But from the reader's point of view, the writer and the physical text he produces can be considered a constant. What we need to explain at this point is what brings different text segments into focal position in different ways so that constants such as the text and the repertoire create a variable entity, the virtual work.

The answer must lie with the fourth factor in the rhetorical transaction: the rhetorical situation. Lloyd Bitzer defines the rhetorical situation as a combination of the audience, the external constraints that govern decision (such as beliefs, documents, facts, traditions, and the like), and the exigence, the imperfection in the current state of affairs that gives rise to the need for discourse in order to set it right.[34] In the case of efferent reading, the reader reads not just for the proximate goal of constructing a meaning from a text, but for the ultimate goal of participating in a conversation in order to update and modify both his own knowledge and that of others. In this context the exigence that gives rise to this participation in a conversation is a general need to make knowledge through discourse. This need is not always precipitated by a specific social occasion, an "imperfection marked by urgency" as Bitzer puts it. Rather it is precipitated by a general awareness that one's structure of beliefs does not perfectly reflect the world as it really is and ought to be.

The reading I have done for this book, for instance, was precipitated first by a vague sense that I did not know enough about teaching the research paper, then by a growing awareness that I did not know enough about reading in general, and then an awareness that I did not know enough about matters such as the function of schemata or the wandering viewpoint. To focus on the last piece of reading cited, I have read Bitzer a number of times before, but I have never before paid attention to the ways in which his definition of the rhetorical situation could help explain variations in interpretation. My own wandering viewpoint was attracted to different aspects of Bitzer's text in the present rhetorical situation: the awareness of gaps in my own knowledge that resulted in researching and writing this book.

Rand Spiro illustrates this point when he notes that many experiments in discourse comprehension present only a text with no purpose:

> One of the main reasons in everyday life for relating new knowledge to old is negated: selectively processing information in order to update one's knowledge (that is, keeping the knowledge "current") of issues which are personally interesting or important. It would be foolish to update one's knowledge with the useless, isolated, and probably false information usually found in experimental prose.[35]

This observation not only undercuts such experiments but underscores the importance of rhetorical exigence as a factor in interpretation.

The rhetorical exigence, then, consists largely of a question or questions. In a sense it is an extension of the traditional rhetorical concept of "stasis." Theories of stasis, first systematized by Hermogenes in the second century and elaborated in the Roman rhetorics of Cicero and Quintilian, hold that the starting point of a rhetorical transaction is not just the rhetor's thesis, but rather the question that must be addressed in order to reach a judgment. As John Gage notes, "Conclusions can be discovered, knowledge can be created in rhetorical discourse, only in the context of an issue which requires deliberation to answer."[36] For forensic rhetoric, the traditional fundamental questions are those articulated by Cicero: "What action occurred?" (fact), "What sort of action was it?" (definition), and "Was it justified?" (quality). For efferent reading, the fundamental question is "What sorts of information and judgments must I add to my system of beliefs in order to bring it nearer to perfection?" From this overarching question the reader can generate all the specific subquestions that govern the route she will take through a developing representation of a text.

To return to Perelman and Olbrechts-Tyteca's formulation, from the reader's point of view, presence is conferred on textual elements and on entire texts, not just by an interaction between text and reader, but by their relevance to the current rhetorical exigence—what the reader wants to know. Under the impetus of a new rhetorical situation, texts read casually and in a linear fashion months or years previously may be sought out and reread, often piecemeal, as the reader mines them for relevant information. Passages that once were skimmed over because they did not obviously relate to any purpose of the reader's now become luminous with meaning. While reading one work, the piece of text in current focus—the "theme," to use Iser's term—may trigger an association with another piece of the same text or a different one, read last week or last month. With no direct textual stimulus at all, pieces of remembered text—that is, pieces of the virtual work—rise to mind at the dinner table, in the shower, at red lights, and are contemplated for their relevance to the current project. The entire constellation of relevant texts becomes a virtual work within which the reader moves freely, but not at random.

The reader's repertoire can be similarly activated by the rhetorical situation. Considered as a total store of schemata, this repertoire may be relatively stable. However, the schemata that matter are the ones made present for the moment by the rhetorical situation—the ones that appear to bear on the question at issue and on the text segments that are currently being contemplated in search of answers to that question. This much smaller store of relevant schemata can shift much more rapidly than the entire structure of the repertoire. Changing it is not a matter of learning new knowledge and accommodating to it; it is simply a matter of shifting attention. Moreover, the act of reading itself is a force that modifies the structure of present schemata, for the knowledge gained while reading must be considered part of the repertoire. However, it is not simply submerged in the great ocean of knowledge that forms the more or less stable mass of the total repertoire. Endowed with relatively greater presence by relevance and temporal proximity, it is more apt to contribute to the much smaller and more specific part of the repertoire that is brought to bear on the immediate inquiry. The relative impact of the new knowledge in this reduced context is therefore proportionally greater than its impact on the total repertoire. In short, then, while the total repertoire must be considered a constant, the part that is currently made present by the rhetorical exigence is much more variable.

The questions that drive the activation of the repertoire and the movement of the wandering viewpoint are of course unstable themselves. The very act of acquiring answers, or partial answers, to some questions inevitably throws up new ones. This is like the well-established concept of the "research cycle": the reader, armed with a very general question, explores sources to find answers that modify and refine the question, which leads him to different sources and back into the same sources with a new focus. This common-sense notion has empirical support: Kantz, for instance, cites research that suggests that "judgments of relevance may change during rereadings, as readers learn more about the problem."[37] But the wandering viewpoint puts a new edge on this old idea. It suggests that the reader's questions guide not just which texts he will go to, but how he evokes a virtual work from those texts. For in Perelman and Olbrechts-Tyteca's formulation, "presence" is dynamic. Textual elements do not just either have or not have presence; they may have it in greater and lesser degree and may acquire it and lose it according to the progress of a rhetorical transaction. This means that as the questions that form the rhetorical exigence shift, the degree of presence conferred upon different aspects of the text shifts with it, causing the network of interrelationships that comprises the virtual work to assume ever new forms. The same text under the constructive gaze of the same reader whose store of questions has been modified will be interrogated differently and a different work will be evoked from it.

Constraints on Construction: The Writer and the Text

The reader's repertoire and the rhetorical situation help explain variations of interpretation. However, if this model is going to be a *rhetorical* model, it must be able to explain not only variation but also limits on variation. As I noted in chapter 1, any rhetorical act is conducted for the purpose of connecting a rhetor and an audience. The rhetorical reader does not simply construe the meaning of a text in space. The meaning of a text is only important insofar as it embodies the meanings of another self—the writer. The reader will sample these meanings to see if any of them are sufficiently believable and forceful that they are worth adding to his own system of beliefs. The writer, of course, has control over the *text*, considered as physical code on paper. But in order for reading to be part of a true conversation, we must ask whether the writer and the text he creates can have any real influence on the shape of the evoked work. In other words, we must ask whether the variations in the repertoire and the rhetorical situation completely deprive a writer of influence over the reader. Can a reader make a text mean anything he wants, and if not, why not?

Some critics answer this question with a qualified "yes." Cleanth Brooks warned us all years ago to beware the "intentional fallacy," that is, supposing that a writer's intention is important to interpretation. More recently, David Bleich has explicitly denied that the author's original intention has any significant effect on the interpreter. Discussing Freud's analysis of Michelangelo's *Moses*, Bleich argues that Freud's interpretation "explains the effect on Freud, *regardless of the artist's intention*. That is, the interpretation explains the interpreter's 'intention'—his perception of and response to the work of art."[38] For Bleich, then, the artist's intention has no relevance to the reader's interpretation; all that is relevant is the interpreter's *perception* of this intention, which is entirely internal to the reader.

Likewise, Fish's theory of interpretive communities suggests that there are no absolute constraints on the meaning of a text. Although he argues that meaning is constrained by the interpretive communities available to create it, he poses no overall constraints on interpretive communities. Absolutely any form of interpretive community has the potential to come into being; there is no way for an author to know or even guess the rules of the game that will be played when others come to construct the meaning of his work. Whereas Bleich simply dismisses the author's intention as irrelevant to the sort of analysis he is interested in, Fish poses a theory that, by depriving the author of the ability to predict his audience, severs the rhetorical link between author and reader. In short, it makes rhetoric impossible.

Others disagree. In *A Rhetoric of Fiction*, for example, Wayne Booth insists most strongly that the voice of an implied author can be heard in texts, and that this implied author is an echo, however distant, of the real, flesh-and-blood author.[39] Linda Flower asserts the same on the basis of research studies involving talk-aloud protocols of readers reading:

> Inferences about the writer's intentions appear to be an essential building block—one that readers actively use to construct a meaningful text. Because readers are participants in a rhetorical situation in which communications have a purpose, recognizing or attempting to infer those intentions is, indeed, a reasonable response.[40]

This observation that readers construct writers will become particularly important in the next chapter, in which I will discuss the way readers evaluate meanings. At this point, however, it still begs the essential question of how it is that we can support theoretically the assertion—so obvious to common sense—that these inferred intentions have anything whatever to do with the author's real intentions.

To answer this question we must first consider standards by which we judge rhetorical connection. In *Modern Dogma*, Wayne Booth argues that logical positivism has "saddled us with standards of truth under which no man can live."[41] To be able to say we have any knowledge at all, he argues, we must set the standard of knowledge lower, so that the variable, contingent understanding that rhetoric produces can still merit the label "knowledge." We must do the same with interpretation. We can never be sure that we know exactly what another means, and the other can never be sure she knows that we know.

Misunderstandings, major and minor, happen to all of us every day; we do not need literary critics to tell us that discourse is often imperfect. In the matter of intention especially, we are often frightened off any notion of theorizing intention because intention, once pushed past simplistic notions of single unified purposes, always reveals itself to be what Flower calls a "bubbling stew" of complex, interwoven, and sometimes contradictory purposes. When my wife tells me to shut the door, I know that she doesn't mean to open the window, but I am not always sure whether she is being critical, ironic, or simply cold. No wonder we sometimes have trouble with Kant. But if we set ourselves rhetorical rather than ideal standards—that is, if we can be content with a mixture of determinacy and indeterminacy—we do not have to assume that because discourse often goes wrong, it never goes right, or at least, right enough to get by on. We can begin to build models to explain *why* we have such a persistent conviction that we often know more or less what each other intends to mean.

Much of this model is already latent in the account of variability that I have already constructed. The repertoire is composed of both public and private elements. The writer cannot predict the most totally private of these elements, the personal associations that are features of the

reader's individual biography. But other elements of the reader's repertoire are far less personal and far more predictable. The reader's schemata, for instance, may in one sense be viewed as personal contributions
to meaning, since they exist within the reader and result from the
reader's personal experience of the work and of discourse conventions.
Yet the experiences on which they are based are not unique to the
individual; they are likely to be similar in many important respects to
those of others. This is so because the most important feature of schema-
based theories of comprehension is the view that knowledge is not
primarily stored—or at any rate, not used in comprehension—as raw
records of personal experience. Rather, it is abstracted into schemata that
are not specific or rigid. We could not possibly have enough rigid
schemata to assimilate all of the diverse experiences we meet every day,
nor could we access them efficiently enough to make sense of our world
in time to deal with it. Therefore, Rumelhart and Ortony argue, schemata
must be quite general: "Schemata attempt to represent knowledge in the
kind of flexible way which reflects human tolerance for vagueness,
imprecision, and quasi-inconsistencies."[42] The specific details of experience tend to be assimilated into patterns of varying degrees of generality,
some of which may be as general as schemata for receiving, breaking,
asking, etc.

Because of this abstractness, the author can depend on these structures to be reasonably well shared between himself and his readers. The
experience of what it means to get together with friends for a game of
cards or a night of playing music is, in broad outline, available to
everyone in a given culture. Only if a culture were to shift to such a degree
that there were *no* points of contact between writer and reader could
communication become impossible. As I noted earlier, it is difficult to
imagine a definition of "culture" broad enough to admit of this degree
of variability. It is this degree of shareability that permits critics such as
Iser to speak of this repertoire as being "in" the text.

This belief in shared universals is a foundation stone of rhetorical
criticism. Kenneth Burke, for instance, states:

> The various kinds of moods, feelings, emotions, perceptions, sensa-
> tions, and attitudes discussed in the manuals of psychology and
> exemplified in works of art, we consider universal experiences. . . .
> We call them universal because all men, under certain conditions,
> and when not in mental or physical collapse, are capable of experi-
> encing them.[43]

Rosenblatt points to another, related element of the repertoire that is
not infinitely unstable. For her, an acceptable interpretation is one that
contains nothing that contradicts the verbal meanings of the text. These

meanings form the stable foundation on which the evoked work is erected, and it achieves this stability by virtue of the fact that the basic meanings of words in a language, however colored by personal overtones and association, do not change from writer to reader to the extent that they become unrecognizable. Knowledge of generally accepted meanings of words forms an element of the reader's repertoire that is relatively stable, shared, and predictable.

This belief in a foundation of stable meaning has received serious challenges from structuralist and particularly poststructuralist criticism. Beginning with Saussure's declaration that the attachment between words and things is totally arbitrary, this body of theory proceeds to the well-known conclusion that all terms in a language are defined only against other terms, and that the distinctions thus produced are themselves arbitrary. The categories into which we segment our world, categories that seem so real to naive introspection, are actually imposed on us by our language, not the other way around. It follows that there is therefore no linguistic basis for assuming that there is such a thing as a substratum of verbal meanings in a text.

Of course this is correct if we are looking for totally invariant meanings. But if we set our sights lower, as I have argued we must in the rhetorical realm of the contingent, we must surely be struck by the remarkable similarities as well as the differences between one person's set of categories and another's, even when the people are from different cultures. And linguistic theory, which caused a lot of the trouble in the first place, offers a principled account of why this should be so, if we look beyond Saussure's informative but now outmoded principles to more modern attempts to grapple with the problem of how we derive our meanings. Theories of natural categories and prototypes suggest that the categories on which words are based, though flexible, are not totally arbitrary. Eleanor Rosch, in particular, has argued that word meanings are stored as generalized prototypes similar in many respects to the generalized outlines of experience that have been labelled "schemata." That is, we have a mental picture of a "most typical" chair, a "most typical" bird, etc. These prototypical forms are not arbitrary (nor are they stored in heaven, as Plato argued). Rather, they are formed according to the probability that certain features will co-occur in the natural world of human experience. Feathers are more likely to co-occur with features such as beaks and wings than with teeth and fins. The prototypical "bird" will combine the maximum number of these objectively probable features. Less typical birds—turkeys, kiwis, ostriches—will possess some but not all of these features.[44] The upshot for a rhetorical theory of reading is that the world of words is indeed based on a world of things.

Consequently, the writer has the right to expect that the denotations of his words will not change to the extent that his most basic meanings will be obscured.

The verbal meanings of the text in turn set limits on possible interpretations, whatever interpretive communities may arise. In discourse processing terms, comprehension is not only "concept-driven" or "top-down," that is, dependent on top-level schemata for the entire construction of meaning. It is simultaneously "data-driven" or "bottom-up," dependent on the minutiae of the text, the verbal meanings on which Rosenblatt depends so heavily, to activate subschema and call into being the high-level interpretive structures that organize meaning as a whole.[45] *Hamlet* admits of a stunningly wide range of interpretations, but if a reader insists that it is about a drunken sailor (or if, as Fish suggests, a reader insists that *A Rose for Emily* is about Eskimos), the verbal level of the text will insist that this meaning is wrong. It will be so out of step with the denotations of the words on the page that it will not be *shareable*, which is one of the most important criteria for calling an interpretation "right." It is always possible, as Fish points out, that information may turn up that permits these interpretations to arise on a symbolic level; we may find out that Faulkner was obsessed with Eskimos, for instance. But these interpretations cannot arise without information about the author's possible intentions to motivate them, information that must be entered into the readers' shared repertoires. In short, differences in repertoire mean that interpretations will vary. But we still cannot hallucinate a text.

The other factor that I have identified as a variable in the rhetorical transaction is the rhetorical situation, that is, the reader's unanswered questions, the gaps in her knowledge that she undertakes the activity of reading in order to fill. This element is similarly predictable. We have been looking at the rhetorical situation from the reader's point of view, but the concept was originally developed to describe the rhetor's understanding of the context of his discourse, an understanding that he can use to systematize the rhetorical decisions that he must make while constructing his text. As imported into a rhetoric of reading, the concept of rhetorical situation does not entirely lose this character of being a set of circumstances about which the writer can have knowledge. A writer knows some of the sorts of questions that her text is intended to answer, for she knows something about the portion of the human conversation in which it is intended to take its place. Each part of that conversation revolves about certain questions that occupy a certain discipline at a certain period of history, and the writer who understands the ongoing conversation in which her work will be read can predict—though without certainty—the general shape of the questions that readers will be using her text to answer. Therefore the rhetorical exigency, which I have identified as a factor permitting variability of interpretation, is nonetheless a partially predictable factor that the writer can take account of in constructing her text. Like the repertoire itself, it is a mixture of public and private—the public conversation and the private route to knowledge that the reader takes as he contemplates various texts and text segments in the light of his personal inquiry after knowledge.

In addition to the shared sections of the reader's repertoire and the rhetorical situation, the writer knows one more thing about the reader that perhaps more than any other factor enables the writer to predict the reader's evocation of the work. Overarching the entire project of evoking a virtual work is the principle of consistency. Rosenblatt sees this principle as providing the foundation for the organizing activity of the reader. Underneath all of the business of evoking the poem as an event in time "is the assumption that the text offers the basis for a coherent experience."[46] The work evoked from the text is not necessarily the same for every reader, but for every reader it is, or it approximates, an "interrelated or interwoven 'whole' or structure."[47] This provides the reader with a predictable goal in reading: to select from the text and from her personal repertoire, not just any elements that strike her fancy, but the elements that will provide the basis for this unified, coherently structured virtual work.

Similarly, Iser writes that "consistency-building is the indispensable basis for all acts of comprehension."[48] The reader constantly brings together perspectives to form gestalts that approach closure to the degree that they are internally consistent. Iser also argues that literature contains a countermovement in which consistency is systematically disrupted by the action of textual blanks. However, whether or not we accept this assertion as being true of literature, Iser himself does not claim that it is true of expository texts; the expository text "aims to fulfill its specific intention in relation to a specific, given fact by observing coherence in order to guarantee the intended reception."[49] For efferent reading at least, then, Iser essentially agrees with Rosenblatt that the reader strives not to build just any evoked work, but rather one that is maximally coherent.

The same search for consistency is posited by discourse-processing theory. Schema are activated when they appear consistent with the text and with the subschema that are already active. An inability to find such consistency triggers a search for schema that are more successful at providing it. We can see this happening as subjects attempted to interpret the music-night/card-game text referred to earlier. Faced with ambiguous or peculiar representations of experience, subjects attempted to find schemata that would account for the elements of the text by building a unified narrative in which the ambiguous words ("score," "recorder," "diamonds") were assigned denotations that all made sense as part of the same schema. Loose ends—unassimilated pieces of data that would not fit the schema—caused consternation:

> Subjects tended to at least attempt to preserve the ambiguity of the original passages. When this did not seem possible, subjects were not reluctant to make their frustrations known: "I found this passage incredibly confusing as I felt the terminology was misleading and misused and therefore I had to reread many times and guess at what was trying to be said. Example: You don't 'listen to' a score."[50]

This expectation of consistency building is perhaps the most important means by which the writer can predict uptake and thereby retain his thread of rhetorical connection with the reader. Even if he does not know the constituents of the reader's total repertoire, he knows that the ones that will be activated are the ones that will be the most consistent with the verbal meanings of the text and with each other. The reader, will if possible, discard inconsistent interpretations and favor those that can be brought into concord with each other. (Deconstructive theory, of course, makes the opposite assumption, that texts can never be brought into coherence. However, the purpose of deconstruction is not comprehension but a demonstration that texts cannot be comprehended.)

This means that the writer must look upon the three factors in the transaction—the textual elements he supplies, the predicted rhetorical situation of the reader, and the elements of the repertoire that he can reasonably expect the reader to possess—as materials out of which a coherent whole must be fashioned. By manipulating the one element that is his to control, the text, he can adjust the sort of coherence that it is possible to form. He can, in other words, introduce into the text elements which, in combination with the expected repertoire and situation, make it relatively easier to form a coherent work that conveys the meaning he intends, and relatively more difficult to form other coherences. Unity building, in short, provides an organizational framework for all other materials of construction, a framework that is not infinitely indeterminate.

The reading process, then, is a delicate balance between sources of constructive freedom and forces that seek to constrain meaning. The former comprise the private and variable aspects of the reader's repertoire and situation, the personal associations of words and experiences and the individual path of the wandering viewpoint. The latter comprise the writer's attempt to fulfill his persuasive intention by manipulating the text according to his best estimate of the reader's repertoire and situation, based on the public, communal, and relatively stable aspects of those parts of the rhetorical transaction.

It is this intersection of public and private, of predictability and freedom, that is the natural home of rhetoric. Kenneth Burke points to this fact when he insists that rhetoric lives suspended between the poles of identification and division:

> Identification is compensatory to division. If men were not apart from one another, there would be no need for the rhetorician to proclaim their unity. If men were wholly and truly of one substance, absolute communication would be of man's very essence. It would not be an ideal, as it now is, partly embodied in material conditions and partly frustrated by these same conditions; rather, it would be as natural, spontaneous, and total as with those ideal prototypes of communication, the theologian's angels, or "messengers."[51]

The sources of unpredictability in discourse, the purely private and unique materials and strategies out of which multiple interpretations arise, are the result of the divisions between the members of the human race. But for all of this division, there is also identification through the regularities of the human situation on which the writer can rely for approximate, if not ideal, communication. It is this inevitable mixture of predictability and unpredictability, of identification and division, that in spite of all the frustrations thereby created makes reading such a consummately rhetorical act.

Notes

1. Aristotle, *Rhetoric*, trans. Lane Cooper (Englewood Cliffs: Prentice-Hall, 1932), 11–12.

2. Wayne Booth, *Modern Dogma and the Rhetoric of Assent* (Chicago: University of Chicago Press, 1974), 114.

3. Mary Louise Pratt, *Toward a Speech-Act Theory of Literary Discourse* (Bloomington: Indiana University Press, 1977).

4. Louise Rosenblatt, *The Reader, The Text, The Poem: The Transactional Theory of the Literary Work* (Carbondale: Southern Illinois University Press, 1978), 24–25.

5. See for instance the contradictory interpretations of Wordsworth's "A Slumber Did My Spirit Seal" by New Critics Brooks and Bateson, cited in Rosenblatt, 116.

6. For a survey of ten major theories, see Robert De Beaugrande, "Design Criteria for Process Models of Reading," *Reading Research Quarterly*, 2 (1981): 261–315.

7. Rand J. Spiro, "Constructive Processes in Prose Comprehension and Recall," in *Theoretical Issues in Reading Comprehension: Perspectives from Cognitive Psychology, Linguistics, Artificial Intelligence, and Education*, ed. Rand J. Spiro, Bertram C. Bruce, and William F. Brewer (Hillsdale: Erlbaum, 1980), 270.

8. Roger Shank and Robert Abelson, *Scripts, Plans, Goals and Understanding* (Hillsdale: Erlbaum, 1977), 4.

9. Stanley Fish, *Is There a Text In This Class? The Authority of Interpretive Communities* (Cambridge: Harvard University Press, 1980), 327.

10. Fish, 330–31.

11. Robert Scholes, *Textual Power: Literary Theory and the Teaching of English* (New Haven: Yale University Press, 1985), 157. Scholes's entire chapter entitled "Who Cares about the Text?" is a scathing indictment of Fish's theories and his methods of arriving at them.

12. Rosenblatt, 12.

13. Rosenblatt, 14.

14. Rosenblatt, 17.

15. Wolfgang Iser, *The Act of Reading: A Theory of Aesthetic Response* (Baltimore: Johns Hopkins University Press, 1978), 21.

16. Ernest T. Goetz and Bonnie B. Armbruster, "Psychological Correlates of Text Structure," in *Theoretical Issues in Reading Comprehension: Perspectives from Cognitive Psychology, Linguistics, Artificial Intelligence, and Education*, ed. Rand J. Spiro, Bertram C. Bruce, and William F. Brewer (Hillsdale: Erlbaum, 1980), 202.

17. Frank Smith, *Understanding Reading: A Psycholinguistic Analysis of Reading and Learning to Read*, 2nd ed. (New York: Holt, 1978).

18. Anderson, Richard C., et al., "Frameworks for Comprehending Discourse," *American Educational Research Journal*, 14 (1977): 372.

19. Robert F. Carey and Jerome C. Harste, "Comprehension as Context: Toward Reconsideration of a Transactional Theory of Reading," in *Understanding Readers' Understanding: Theory and Practice*, ed. Robert J. Tierney, Patricia L. Anders, and Judy Nichols Mitchell (Hillsdale: Erlbaum, 1987), 198.

20. Rand J. Spiro, "Constructive Processes in Prose Comprehension and Recall," in *Theoretical Issues in Reading Comprehension: Perspectives from Cognitive Psychology, Linguistics, Artificial Intelligence, and Education*, ed. Rand J. Spiro, Bertram C. Bruce, and William F. Brewer (Hillsdale: Erlbaum, 1980), 245.

21. Iser, 24.

22. Iser, 69.

23. Iser, 143.

24. Kathleen McCormick and Gary E. Waller, "Text, Reader, Ideology: The Interactive Nature of the Reading Situation," *Poetics*, 16 (1987): 193–208.

25. Margaret Kantz, "Toward A Pedagogically Useful Theory of Literary Reading," *Poetics*, 16 (1987): 161.

26. For an overview of recent work in this area, see Nancy Nelson Spivey, "Construing Constructivism: Reading Research in the United States," *Poetics*, 16 (1987): 169–92. The concept of "schemata" is one of the most commonly accepted models of knowledge representation. Others exist, including "frames," which emphasize the static and stereotyped nature of data, and "scripts," which emphasize the way knowledge tends to be stored as stereotyped sequences of events. Gillian Brown and George Yule provide a useful summary of these concepts in *Discourse Analysis* (Cambridge: Cambridge University Press, 1983), 238–50. They point out that these formulations represent not so much competing theories as alternative metaphors for the way knowledge is organized (238).

27. David E. Rumelhart, "Schemata: The Building Blocks of Cognition," in *Theoretical Issues in Reading Comprehension: Perspectives from Cognitive Psychology, Linguistics, Artificial Intelligence, and Education,* ed. Rand J. Spiro, Bertram C. Bruce, and William F. Brewer (Hillsdale: Erlbaum, 1980), 34.

28. Rumelhart, 37.

29. For a discussion of the ways in which schemata are changed through accretion, modification, and restructuring, see Rumelhart, 52–54.

30. Robert de Beaugrande, "Text, Attention, and Memory in Reading Research," in *Understanding Readers' Understanding: Theory and Practice,* ed. Robert J. Tierney, Patricia L. Anders, and Judy Nichols Mitchell (Hillsdale: Erlbaum, 1987), 22–23.

31. See, for instance, Iser, 111 and 185.

32. Iser, 111.

33. Chaim Perelman and L. Olbrechts-Tyteca, *The New Rhetoric: A Treatise on Argumentation,* trans. John Wilkinson and Purcell Weaver (Notre Dame: University of Notre Dame Press, 1969), 117.

34. Lloyd Bitzer, "The Rhetorical Situation," in *Contemporary Theories of Rhetoric: Selected Readings,* ed. Richard L. Johannesen (New York: Harper, 1971), 381–93.

35. Rand J. Spiro, "Remembering Information from Text: The 'State of Schema' Approach," in *Schooling and the Acquisition of Knowledge,* ed. Richard C. Anderson, Rand J. Spiro, and William E. Montague (Hillsdale: Erlbaum, 1977), 140.

36. John T. Gage, "An Adequate Epistemology for Composition: Classical and Modern Perspectives," in *Essays on Classical Rhetoric and Modern Discourse,* ed. Robert J. Connors, Lisa S. Ede, and Andrea A. Lunsford (Carbondale: Southern Illinois University Press, 1984), 158.

37. Kantz, 165.

38. David Bleich, *Subjective Criticism* (Baltimore: Johns Hopkins University Press, 1978), 89.

39. Wayne Booth, *The Rhetoric of Fiction,* 2nd ed. (Chicago: University of Chicago Press, 1983).

40. Linda Flower, "The Construction of Purpose in Writing and Reading," *College English,* 50 (1988): 539.

41. Booth, xii.

42. David E. Rumelhart and Andrew Ortony, "The Representation of Knowledge in Memory," in *Schooling and the Acquisition of Knowledge,* ed. Richard C. Anderson, Rand J. Spiro, and William E. Montague (Hillsdale: Erlbaum, 1977), 111.

43. Kenneth Burke, *Counter-Statement* (Berkeley: University of California Press. 1931), 149.

44. See Eleanor Rosch, "Universals and Cultural Specifics in Human Categorization," in *Cross-Cultural Perspectives on Learning,* ed. Richard W. Brislin, Stephen Bochner, Walker J. Lonner (New York: Sage-Wiley, 1975), 177–206; Eleanor Rosch, et al., "Basic Objects in Natural Categories," *Cognitive Psychology,* 8 (1976): 382–439; Christine C. Pappas, "The Role of 'Typicality' in Reading Comprehension," in *Understanding Readers' Understanding: Theory and Practice,* ed. Robert J. Tierney, Patricia L. Anders, and Judy Nichols Mitchell (Hillsdale:

Erlbaum, 1987), 129–45; Carolyn B. Mervis, "Category Structure and the Development of Categorization," in *Theoretical Issues in Reading Comprehension: Perspectives from Cognitive Psychology, Linguistics, Artificial Intelligence, and Education*, ed. Rand J. Spiro, Bertram C. Bruce, and William F. Brewer (Hillsdale: Erlbaum, 1980), 279–307.

45. See Rumelhart, 41–42, and Rumelhart and Ortony, 128–29.

46. Rosenblatt, 55.

47. Rosenblatt, 91.

48. Iser, 125.

49. Iser, 185.

50. Carey and Harste, 197.

51. Kenneth Burke, *A Rhetoric of Motives* (Berkeley: University of California Press, 1950), 22.

3 From Interpretation to Belief

What Does It Mean to Be Persuaded?

In chapter 2, I outlined a rhetorical account of the first stage in the reading process: the evocation of the virtual work itself. Under the impetus of the questions she wants answered—the rhetorical situation—the reader relates the symbols of the text to her own repertoire of linguistic and world knowledge to construct a virtual work that is as coherent and unified as possible. This virtual work, though a mental construct of the reader, represents the reader's best estimate of the propositions that the writer is attempting to communicate to her. It constitutes a rhetorical channel, a structure of identifications by means of which one human being makes contact with another.

From the rhetorical point of view, however, constructing meanings is only part of the process of exchanging discourse. In order to build knowledge through the rhetorical interchange of meanings, the reader must not only construct but also be affected by the virtual work. She has listened to one previous turn of the unending conversation; now she must decide how much, if any, of what she has heard is worth believing, and with what intensity of conviction. In addition, she must sort out the differing and often opposing claims of other works evoked from other texts, decide whether the theses presented have more merit than the ones that make up her current structure of beliefs, and finally integrate the more meritorious theses into that structure. These two closely related aspects of the reading process generate my third and fourth guiding questions: "How does the reader evaluate the propositions presented by individual texts and decide which to be persuaded by?" and "How does the reader negotiate among the claims of various texts in order to develop a unified system of knowledge?"

Just as it supplied key concepts toward the building of a model of interpretation, discourse-processing theory can help in the building of a model of evaluation. Whereas rhetoric seeks to answer the question, "How should I choose the strategies that will persuade my audience," discourse-processing theory asks a question more closely related to the reception rather than the production of discourse: "What happens when

people do or do not add new knowledge to their developing worldviews?"
Discourse-processing theory, therefore, can help us understand exactly
what we mean when we say that we have been "persuaded" of something.

Texts that seek to persuade us do not simply erect a new structure of
beliefs on vacant ground. They seek not just to create but to *change* our
minds. This means that they start with structures of belief that are
already in place. Each act of rhetoric modifies the worldview that we
already have, convincing us to add certain features to it, to subtract
others as no longer useful or true to our current theory of the world, and
to modify still others to bring about a better fit with reality (or at least,
what we are currently convinced is reality).

Thus characterized, "being persuaded" fits exactly into the domain of
discourse-processing theories of comprehension, theories that see adding to knowledge as a central goal of discourse comprehension. In "The
Notion of Schemata and the Educational Enterprise," Richard C. Anderson summarizes what implications the schematic perspective may have
for our understanding of information acquisition.[1] To describe the way
schemata function, Anderson borrows two terms from Piaget: "assimilation" and "accommodation."[2] We have seen how schemata, the organized stores of knowledge built from a lifetime of experience, help us to
sort out sensory input and turn it into meaning. Anderson calls this
process "assimilation": one's preexisting schemata act as filters, select-
ing the interpretations that can be placed on sensory input and telling us
how to make sense of it. To make an analogy with Fish's terms, they
provide the interpretive framework for the construction of meaning. A
wide variety of research into comprehension processes suggests that the
reader's prior knowledge is an overwhelmingly dominant force in
comprehending texts.[3]

But schemata themselves cannot be fully deterministic (in what
Brown and Yule call the "strong" view of schemata).[4] If they were, they
would force us to see the same things in all data, filtering out what is
novel because it cannot be assimilated to old schemata. This would
prevent the growth of new knowledge. Meaningful epistemic conversation would cease: we would only hear what we already know. Therefore,
there has to be a corresponding movement by which the schemata
themselves are modified to take account of new information with which
they are not already equipped to deal. Anderson, following Piaget, calls
this latter process "accommodation." Schemata continually shift and
adjust to reflect new knowledge as it becomes available, either through
direct sensory input or through the uptake of others' rhetoric. This
process of accommodating one's worldview to take account of argu-

ments presented to one—that is, the process of changing one's mind for good reasons—is the ultimate goal of reading considered as a rhetorical process.

Being persuaded thus involves a delicate push-pull balance between assimilation and accommodation. To the extent that we assimilate new knowledge to old, we will fail to be persuaded in any meaningful way. We may add some units of data to our store of knowledge, but we will not make any changes in the system of beliefs that organizes those data. To the extent that we accommodate our worldview to the new knowledge that is being offered us, we will be persuaded. The extreme case of assimilation is a total failure to learn or to progress; the extreme case of accommodation, mental anarchy. To avoid either of these pathological extremes, rhetorical uptake must consist of a balance between assimilation and accommodation, between filtering our perceptions through old experience and taking account of new.

This model of persuasion, based on Anderson's model of assimilation and accommodation, provides us with a more specific and more answerable version of the question, "What happens when we are persuaded?" The question is focused to a search for the factors that control this balance between assimilation and accommodation—that is, the factors that answer Booth's question, "When should I change my mind?"

The question is complicated by the fact that to change one's mind is not a simple yes/no decision. Presented with arguments that conflict with one's currently existing beliefs, one does not simply choose between rejecting the arguments or modifying the beliefs. One can modify one's belief system in more than one direction, incorporating into it some elements of one text, some of another, and some that are entirely new constructions triggered by the discussion in which one is engaged but not explicitly found in any one of the texts that clamor for attention. Moreover, one's attitude to a particular text is always influenced by implied comparisons, conscious or unconscious, with other texts in the conversation. An argument that might be fully convincing by itself may appear in a completely different light when set beside other arguments that compete with it. One's personal belief system, then, is a dynamic balance of a number of opposing forces, each attempting to alter the system's precarious coherence in a different direction.

Thus, changing one's mind is not a matter of choosing from a variety of texts the one that is the most persuasive and then accepting it. Rather, it is a matter of assigning the propositions presented by all texts an appropriate place in an intricate system. Some will be rejected completely. Others will be accepted in part: some features of the worldview they offer will be incorporated into the reader's own system while others will not. Still others will promote not so much an addition or subtraction of specific features of that worldview as a relative weakening or strengthening of the degree of confidence placed in those features. As Sperber and Wilson argue in *Relevance: Communication and Cognition*, "Improvements in our representation of the world can be achieved not only by adding justified new assumptions to it, but also by appropriately raising or lowering our degree of confidence in them."[5] Or more succinctly from Perelman and Olbrechts-Tyteca, "What is characteristic of the adherence of minds is its variable intensity."[6]

What, then, are the critical factors in the "logic of relative weight" (as Booth calls it) that readers use to decide which texts will receive more and which less relative weight in the final synthesis? Or in terms of the discourse-processing model, what decides whether new material will be assimilated to preexisting structures or will provoke an accommodation in the system, rearranging the schema through which the perceiver interprets reality?

Discourse-processing theories of comprehension offer us a useful model of the mental structures that are modified by persuasion. However, by their very nature as theories of *comprehension*, discourse-processing theories address only tangentially the question of how the reader reaches this judgment. In other words, while offering fairly well-developed theories of how people decide *what* is being said, these theories are somewhat less helpful in explaining how people decide whether or not to believe it—that is, how they are persuaded to make significant accommodations in their structure of beliefs on the basis of new information. Anderson admits that the processes involved in answering the latter question, essentially a question of how schemata themselves change, are still poorly understood.[7] In her paper "Cognitive Development and the Acquisition of Concepts," Katherine Nelson makes a similar admission: "Most of what we know about knowledge at any stage of development has to do with its content and structure rather than how it is acquired."[8] The assimilation/accommodation model, in short, offers a valuable characterization of the general process of being persuaded, but does not fill in the details of what influences that process. In Nelson's words, it "resists concretizing."

One way to concretize this process is to recognize it as a version of the rhetorical problem of reaching a judgment. To reach a judgment on a question is to reach a decision as to whether a certain proposition or set of propositions is at least provisionally worth incorporating into one's own structure of beliefs. The entire business of philosophical rhetoric is to understand persuasive processes in order to specify how the rhetor, through words alone, can influence the judgments of his hearers. Rhetorical theory offers a highly specific account of how it is that hearers reach judgments under the influence of discourse.

One of the most fundamental and long-standing features of this rhetorical account of judgment is the three *pisteis* or modes of proof. Aristotle defines these modes as follows:

> Of the means of persuasion supplied by the speech itself there are three kinds. The first kind reside in the character of the speaker; the second consist in producing a certain attitude in the hearer; the third appertain to the argument proper, in so far as it actually or seemingly demonstrates.[9]

These are the well-known classical modes of proof that are commonly called ethos (persuasion based on the perceived character of the speaker), pathos (persuasion based on appeal to the audience's emotions), and logos (persuasion based on reasoned arguments).

In one form or another, these three modes persistently reappear in rhetorics down to the present day. They formed a vital part of Roman rhetorics such as those of Cicero and Quintilian. In the early days of Christian rhetoric, they appeared in the rhetorical theories of St. Augustine, who insisted that emotional proof, and particularly the testimony of the speaker's own character, should accompany reasoned evidence. During the eighteenth and nineteenth centuries, this three-part division acquired a more specific psychological basis, for the psychology of the day saw the human mind as divided into discrete faculties such as reason, sympathy, the emotions, and the will. This division provided a basis for rhetoricians such as Campbell and Whately to identify the modes of proof with more or less absolute divisions in the human psyche. Modern psychology provides no such clear-cut basis for this division, but Aristotle's original distinction continues to provide a useful means of discussing types of evidence. Booth, for instance, argues that to rehabilitate rhetoric, the modern fixation on logical proof must be tempered by a revival of pathetic and ethical evidence.[10] Richard Weaver, also arguing for a more humane and efficacious rhetoric, explicitly casts his argument back to classical rhetoricians such as Quintilian in order to argue that the human being is not merely a thinking machine, but rather a composite being that responds both to the ethical properties of the orator—a man who is "good in his formed character and right in his ethical philosophy"—and to his feelings, "the activity in him most closely related to what used to be called his soul."[11]

The division of proof into three modes, then, comes to us sanctioned by a long history of both technical rhetorics such as Cicero's, in which it is recommended because it seems to work, and philosophical rhetorics from Aristotle to Weaver, in which it is recommended because it recognizes the complexity of the human being as a creature that naturally responds to reason, emotion, and social example. This venerable scheme can be useful again here. A terminology obliges us to make certain distinctions when applying it. Using the three modes of proof to describe rhetorical reading focuses attention on the fact that being persuaded is an integrated activity that partakes of at least three different aspects of the human being: her cognitive capacity to apply rules of evidence, her tendency to be influenced by her emotions, and her pull in the direction of ideas that are presented by those whose character she values. It is this integrated approach that can take the model beyond the cognitive orientation of discourse-processing theory and into the more multifaceted realm of rhetoric.

How Texts Persuade: The Logical Dimension

Let us begin with logos in its most basic classical form. The heart of Aristotle's system of logos is the enthymeme. The enthymeme is the rhetorical equivalent of the syllogism, in which a conclusion is automatically entailed by two premises. In the most basic form of the syllogism, a generalization such as "All men are mortal" (the major premise) is connected to a specific conclusion such as "Socrates is mortal" by means of a particular fact that bridges the two, such as "Socrates is a man" (minor premise). When used rhetorically as an enthymeme, this form of logical argument may be expressed without one or the other of its premises being made explicit, for these premises may be obvious to the audience and repeating them would be merely tedious. An enthymeme based on the above syllogism might be, "Socrates is mortal because he is a man"; the major premise is too obvious to the audience to need stating. The enthymeme is also distinguished from the syllogism by the fact that its premises and therefore its conclusions may be only probable. The justice system, for instance, makes profitable use of premises such as "A person with motivation to commit a crime is more likely to have actually committed one than is a person who has no motivation." This premise is far from certain, but without recourse to such uncertain premises, we could not get along in the uncertain world we must live in. The enthymeme is thus a device drawn from demonstrative logic but adapted to the needs of rhetoric, an art, not of absolute formal relationships, but of human interaction in the realm of the contingent.

Because it is rooted in human interaction, an enthymeme must be constructed, Aristotle notes, "not from any and every premise that may be regarded as true, but from opinions of a definite sort—the opinions of the judges, or else the opinions of persons whose authority they accept."[12] Unlike the syllogism, then, the enthymeme is not simply a logical device but a device by which the rhetor establishes contact with the audience by arguing from the opinions that they already hold. Classical rhetoricians called these opinions *doxai*. The classical term is a useful one because, unlike "opinion," which suggests a rather casual and possibly unsubstantiated point of view on a particular subject, it suggests a kind of knowledge. Doxai are less certain than *episteme*, demonstrable deductive knowledge, but they represent knowledge nonetheless—the flickering, insubstantial knowledge of this contingent world with which rhetoric must always dirty its hands.

In order to make use of this technique, the rhetor must know how to find both general and particular doxai with which to build his enthymemes. Accordingly, Aristotle provides lists of topics (*topoi*) to which the rhetor can turn for material. The special topics (*eide*) are those which are specific to certain fields, especially ethics, law, and politics. Under these headings, Aristotle provides lists, not of specific facts—for that is the province of the individual arts themselves, not of rhetoric—but of areas of knowledge in which the rhetor must be informed. These include matters of government, national defence, and economics, together with the basics of psychology such as the sources of human motivation, and general ethical matters such as the sources of virtue. The general or common topics (*koinoi topoi*), on the other hand, are general principles of argument which can be used to generate discourse in any discipline. As Grimaldi puts it, they are "forms of inference into which syllogistic, or enthymematic, reasoning naturally falls."[13] They provide the logical shape which may be applied to the particular facts of the special topics in order to produce arguments for a particular occasion. Two lists of such topics appear in the *Rhetoric*: a list of twenty-eight detailed lines of argument such as definition, division, precedent, and consequences, and a list of four highly generalized topoi: possible and impossible, more and less, past fact and future fact. The common topic of more and less, for instance, embraces all arguments from comparison. When applied to the specific material of the special topics, the concept of more and less produces generalizations such as the following:

> Those things are greater in which superiority is more desirable or nobler. Thus keen sight is more desirable than a keen sense of smell, since sight itself is more desirable than the sense of smell; and since it is nobler to surpass in loving one's friends than in loving money, love of one's friends is itself nobler than the love of money.[14]

These two major components of logos—the enthymeme and the topoi—reappear in various forms throughout the history of rhetoric.[15] In *The New Rhetoric*, for instance, Perelman and Olbrechts-Tyteca provide a copious and detailed discussion of loci of argument such as identity, definition, ends and means, waste, analogy, and dissociation of concepts, a list strikingly like Aristotle's twenty-eight common topoi in general design if not in detail. Perelman and Olbrechts-Tyteca also echo Aristotle's insistence that the premises of argument must be chosen from premises accepted by the audience:

> The unfolding as well as the starting point of the argumentation presuppose indeed the agreement of the audience. This agreement is sometimes on explicit premises, sometimes on the particular connecting links used in the argument or on the manner of using these links: from start to finish, analysis of argumentation is concerned with what is supposed to be accepted by the hearers.[16]

This insight recaptures and redevelops the heart of the Aristotelian enthymeme: the linking of an argument to doxai, the preexisting agreements of the audience.

Ancient and modern examples of logos could be multiplied indefinitely. The important question here is, what components of this rhetorical approach to logical argument can help explain how we judge the theses presented to us by the writers we read?

Recall that one of the primary features of the rhetorical model of reading is the role played by the reader's repertoire of experience, much of it gained through prior interaction with texts. This repertoire acts as a filter, causing new knowledge to be assimilated to the schemata set up by the old. This implies the question of how new knowledge provokes the opposite reaction, causing the schemata to be accommodated to it. How does new knowledge break through the barriers, the "terministic screens," to use Burke's term, that would seem to exclude it?

The principles of logos suggest that new information is connected to old through bridging generalizations. These generalizations are already accepted by the audience but are activated—"made present" in Perelman and Olbrechts-Tyteca's terms—by the rhetor's language. An important point is that this account emphasizes the *selective* nature of the argumentative process. The reader's structure of knowledge may be a coherent and interrelated system, but that does not mean that it is an inseparable monolith. Rather, it is a mass of related but separate generalizations, each of which individually may become the premise for an argument when a piece of discourse gives it presence by so using it.

Take, for instance, a person who is reading various authorities in pursuit of the answers to a problem—say, understanding how to use collaborative writing in the classroom. First she reads Thomas Johnson's vigorous denunciation of collaborative writing because of its potential to destroy the sovereignty of the individual.[17] Then she reads John Trimbur's later article, "Consensus and Difference in Collaborative Learning," a defense of collaborative learning that replies to a number of specific criticisms against the practice, including explicitly Thomas Johnson's.[18] (In chapter 4, I will examine an extended conversation of this type in considerable detail; here I just want to propose a hypothetical account of a reader trying to negotiate between two conflicting texts to illustrate a more limited point.) If the dispute between Johnson and Trimbur were a simple matter of one making a claim and the other saying the opposite, we could predict one of two responses on the part of the reader. She might decide between them on the basis of which connected the most obviously with her own preexisting beliefs. If she believed most strongly in individualism, she would believe Johnson, and if she believed most strongly in consensus, she would believe Trimbur. In either case, she would have added some basic units of information to her knowledge—she would know more about exactly how collaborative learning did or did not enhance one of these goals—but she would not have been fundamentally changed in any meaningful way. She would have assimilated one position and filtered out the other, and accommodated her beliefs to nothing. The other possibility would be that she would see no means of choosing between the opposing positions and just give up.

Considered as a whole, then, a system of beliefs cannot be changed by an incoming argument any more than a person can pull himself up by his own bootstraps. But if the beliefs are considered as separable *doxai* rather than an unbreakable structure, it then becomes possible for certain of them to be used as premises for an argument the conclusion of which involves the changing of *other* doxai. As Kenneth Burke puts it, "Some of their [the audience's] opinions are needed to support the fulcrum by which he [the rhetor] would move other opinions."[19]

In the example above, the dispute between Johnson and Trimbur is not simply a matter of one affirming and the other denying a single claim (like John Cleese's famous Monty Python argument: "Yes, I did." "No, you didn't." "You're just contradicting me." "No, I'm not.") Nor is the reader's judgment based on the application of a single doxa, such as a preference for individualism over consensus. Rather, each position is a complex of beliefs. Trimbur, for instance, defends collaborative learning by appealing through Bruffee back to his sources in Dewey, arguing that a desire to privilege individualism is, in effect, an attempt to keep students as atomistic individuals and prevent their forming the authority that comes of group interaction. If the reader is convinced by this argument, it will be because she believes that, in general, groups are stronger than individuals, and that it is beneficial for students to have the authority that comes of group strength. This is not quite the same as merely tuning in to preexisting beliefs (such as a belief in consensus or individualism) as a block. Some of her opinions will have been used to support the fulcrum by which the rhetor will have moved others. In the process, a modified view of group interaction will have come into being. The reader will not have overhauled her entire system of beliefs, but will have accommodated some to the new relationships that the author has pointed out to her.

This viewpoint allows us to explain more clearly not only why arguments work but also why they sometimes fail to work, even when, from the rhetor's point of view, they are constructed as well as they possibly could be. In "Attitudes, Beliefs, and Information Acquisition," Robert S. Wyer, Jr. addresses this problem from the viewpoint of discourse-processing theory:

> It seems likely that the implications of new information will be resisted if its acceptance would require a major cognitive reorganization, that is, if it would require a change in a large number of other logically related beliefs in order to maintain consistency among them.[20]

The rhetorical perspective on logos allows us to put this another way. The important factor is not simply the total degree of cognitive reorganization that would be required in order to accommodate to—that is, to be persuaded by—a given argument. Rather, all other factors being equal, an argument will succeed to the extent that the opinions it evokes as premises are more deeply held than those that would be changed by its acceptance. In the above case, the reader will be convinced if (say) her belief in the two premises Trimbur uses—that groups are stronger than individuals and that students ought to have authority—is stronger than opposing beliefs such as a distrust of consensus.

We cannot, of course, know what opinions each reader will hold more deeply than others. But in general, more deeply held opinions, ones that can best be used as fulcra to move others, are the fundamental relationships among things described by the common topoi. The topic of possible/impossible, for instance, predicts that a reader who is shown that a particular belief is impossible in the light of other pieces of data that she accepts will generally be induced to accommodate that claim—that is, reject the belief—even though it involves changing a well-entrenched belief structure.

This model is not intended to suggest that all human thought proceeds by means of the formal deductive enthymeme. The enthymeme is only a broadly metaphoric model that formalizes the observation that the ideas evoked from a text must tap into parts of the reader's mental construct in order to influence other parts. A text thus becomes a good reason for changing one's mind, not just on its intrinsic merits such as deductive validity, but also on its merits relative to the audience. It will be a good reason if the doxai it activates as premises are powerful enough to allow it sufficient leverage against the convictions it is attempting to change.

Within this framework a refusal to be persuaded by an apparently irrefutable argument is not necessarily incompetent or pathological. Rather, it is the natural consequence of the interdependence of the beliefs that make up our theory of the world. Our reluctance to change such structures provides a stabilizing effect that ensures that we always have a solid base of belief to act as an interpretive framework without our having to readjust the entire structure to accommodate every new input. The imperceptible gradient from conviction through obsession to neurotic delusion is not a simple matter of willingness or unwillingness to modify belief. Rather it is a matter of degree and of functionality. The system becomes pathological and maladaptive when new arguments that *should* make a conceptual reorganization appear the most desirable response do not in fact do so.

This model is also not intended to suggest that this process of weighing beliefs for their connections to preexisting doxai is always or even frequently conscious. The process of reaching a judgment, like the process of interpreting a text, is almost certainly a largely tacit process, one that proceeds unconsciously most of the time. It must be so, for life presents us with large and small judgments to make all the time, and if we had to evaluate enthymemes consciously every time we discoursed with another person, we would not be able to get on with our lives.

Nonetheless, the art of rhetorical logos, at bottom a study of how arguments may be chosen, can also be used to describe the mechanism by which arguments are accepted or rejected. This account forces us to extend the "information-processing" model offered by discourse-processing theory into an "argument-processing" model. Data does not come into the system simply as isolated bits. Rather, it comes as complex and interrelated systems, embedded in arguments which may or may not connect the input, the specific claims of the writer, to the doxai that make up the preexisting system of beliefs. These systems consist of relationships between specific pieces of world knowledge—what the ancient rhetoricians called the "special topoi"—and more deeply embedded assumptions about relationships—the "common topoi." The reader may accept or reject these arguments or use them in ways not anticipated by the writer, according to the demands of the larger system into which they must be integrated.

How Texts Persuade: The Emotional Dimension

The principle of logos helps explain rhetorical uptake. However, the traditional division of proof into three modes reminds us that logos does not exhaust the means of persuasion. Emotion also plays a key role in forming our beliefs. In popular notions of argument, reliance on emotion is typically dismissed as wrong-headed. "You are just being emotional," we are apt to say. "Why can't you be logical?" But this attitude, which Booth describes as "scientismic," will not get us very far in the real world. In order to explain how people really are persuaded, the art of rhetoric has had to create models of how emotions affect people in a systematic, explainable, and thus at least partly predictable and controllable manner.

Although he does not approve of deliberately attempting to win a case through irrelevant emotional appeals (which he likens to warping a carpenter's rule), Aristotle recognizes that if rhetoric is to be an art of influencing human beings it must take account of all, not just some, of the factors that cause human beings to make the judgments they do:

> The same thing does not appear the same to men when they are friendly and when they hate, nor when they are angry and when they are in gentle mood; in these different moods the same thing will appear either wholly different in kind, or different as to magnitude.[21]

He therefore provides a detailed analysis of the emotions and their connection to various general human types. The rhetorician who understands these aspects of the audience will have the tools required to put that audience in the right frame of mind to receive his enthymemic proofs in a positive light.

Like logos, pathos has been variously reinterpreted throughout the history of rhetoric. Sometimes it has been interpreted strategically, as mainly a technique to be used because it works. Cicero, for instance, recommends using emotional arguments, highly charged language, and even theatrical effects. In *De Oratore*, his character Antonius describes a courtroom scene:

> Assuredly I felt that the Court was deeply affected when I called forward my unhappy old client, in his garb of woe, and when I did those things approved of by yourself, Crassus . . . I mean my tearing open his tunic and exposing his scars. While Gaius Marius, from his seat in court, was strongly reinforcing, by his weeping, the pathos of my appeal, . . . all this lamentation, as well as my invocation of every god and man, every citizen and ally, was accompanied by tears and vast indignation on my own part.[22]

This technical form of pathos set the tone for Roman rhetoric in general, as Johnson notes in "Reader-Response and the *Pathos* Principle":

> Such attention in *De Oratore* (and in other classical works such as the *Ad Herennium* and Quintilian's *Institutio Oratoria*) to definitions of various kinds of audience response and to inventional and stylistic strategies for anticipating, circumventing, and co-opting audience predisposition in the service of persuasion awarded the *pathos* principle a central role in Roman rhetoric and in the long pedagogical tradition that the classical traditions inspired.[23]

This tendency to use pathos as a purely technical means of persuasion has resulted in a long history of rhetorical distrust of emotion. This history can be traced back to Plato's image of the soul as a charioteer drawn up to heaven by the white horse of reason and down to earth by the black horse of the emotions,[24] and forward to the popular distrust of "emotionalism" referred to above. Yet the notion persists that the emotions are also a vital part of the human decision-making system. Richard Weaver states this viewpoint in "Language is Sermonic":

> The most obvious truth about rhetoric is that its object is the whole man. It presents its arguments first to the rational part of man, because rhetorical discourses, if they are honestly conceived, always have a basis in reasoning. . . . Yet it is the very characterizing feature of rhetoric that it goes beyond this and appeals to other parts of man's constitution, especially to his nature as a pathetic being, that is, a being feeling and suffering.[25]

Thus the emotions can be seen not just as a means of doing an end run around rationality, but as a valid source of evidence for knowing. As Booth puts it in *Modern Dogma*, "Every desire, every feeling, can become a good reason when called into the court of symbolic exchange."[26]

This is the aspect of rhetoric that Burke captures in his term "courtship." Men and women are dissimilar beings who must be brought together through the emotional processes of courtship as well as the intellectual processes of argument. Similarly, rhetoric, because it contains within itself the power of pathos, is a more powerful force of identification than is logic alone. Pathos leaps like a spark across the divisions that are inevitable in human society, creating the emotional identifications that allow rhetorical interchange to occur. Thus, says Burke, "Rhetoric remains the mode of appeal essential for bridging the conditions of estrangement 'natural' to society as we know it."[27]

We can see the effects of this emotional source of proof even in the discourse of "hard" scientists. The hard sciences are traditionally supposed to be maximally free of aesthetic and emotional processes. However, in *Opening Pandora's Box*, G. Nigel Gilbert and Michael Mulkay take a much closer look at scientific discourse from a sociological point of view, and reveal the extent to which emotion shapes even scientific judgment. In formal scientific literature, Gilbert and Mulkay point out, theory is presented as if it followed inductively from scientific data. Informal accounts, however, often reveal that theory is arrived at first, in a flash of emotionally charged intuitive insight, and the scientific results collected later by way of confirmation and documentation. One of Gilbert and Mulkay's subjects offers this account of a particular scientific revelation:

> He came running into the seminar, pulled me out along with one of his other post-docs and took us to the back of the room and explained this idea that he had. . . . He was very excited. He was really high. He said, "What if I told you that it didn't take any energy to make ATP at the catalytic site, it took energy to kick it off the catalytic site?" It took him about 30 seconds. But I was particularly predisposed to this idea. Everything I'd been thinking, 12, 14, 16 different pieces of information in the literature that could not be explained, and then all of a sudden the simple explanation became clear. . . . And so we sat down and designed some experiments to prove, test this.[28]

How can we take pathos into account in a rhetorical model of reading? An answer is suggested by the hypothetical reader of Johnson and Trimbur that I constructed earlier. I suggested two possible premises which, when taken together, might lead that reader to accept Trimbur's account over Johnson's: a belief that groups are strong, and a belief that students should have authority. The first of these is clearly a belief in a certain aspect of reality, a generalization about the way things are, or tend to be, in the world. These are the sorts of premises that typically appear in the logical syllogisms on which rhetorical logos is modeled. But the second of these is not a belief in what is, but a belief in what ought to be—not a fact, but a value. Rendered as a bald statement like this, it seems little different in kind from a fact-based premise. However, the convenient propositionalized form in which I have rendered it disguises the fact that beliefs of this type are not generally held as tidy statements that can fit into an enthymeme as a major or minor premise. Rather, they are bundles of general attitudes—fuzzy, usually unstated, often unstatable, and almost always accompanied by emotional overtones. Indeed, the strength of this type of belief can often be measured by the strength of emotional reaction that it provokes when instantiated. One who believes strongly that students must be empowered will react with strong negative emotions to a claim that challenges this belief and with strong positive emotions to a claim that supports it.

The rhetorical point of view insists that these emotions are not simply excrescences, defects of the audience that can be manipulated by the rhetor. Rather, they are inevitable concommitants of a certain type of belief: a belief in the *value* of a proposition. We often base our judgments on the emotional overtones of these values without instantiating the underlying proposition. That is, we may react favorably to an argument that seems to empower students without consciously invoking a premise such as "Students must be empowered." Likewise the audience of Antonius's speech in *De Oratore* (though the theatrics are overdone by modern standards) may legitimately be moved by their sympathy for the scarred veteran without invoking a premise such as "Much respect is due a man who has been wounded in his country's service." The scientist may emotionally apprehend that a theory "has" to be right without invoking a premise to the effect of "An idea that is exciting is more likely to be fruitful than one that is not." Yet each of these premises is backed by its own good reasons—the teacher's premise encapsulates the current social values of a profession, the Roman audience's encapsulates the social values of a civilization, and the scientist's is backed by a lifetime of personal experience in which the emotionally and the intellectually fruitful have generally been commingled. These emotional reactions are necessary shortcuts that get us through our day without having to use our overloaded rational faculties at every point. Like everything else dealt with by rhetoric, each of these premises is uncertain. And like any shortcut, overreliance on emotional reaction can become pathological. Yet our ability to mingle emotional and logical proofs also expresses our humanness. As Booth points out, what we "know" is not just facts; it is a complex of attitudes and perceptions that shapes our selves and gives us our personal identities. Accordingly, a rhetorical model of reading must describe beliefs not just as organized bundles of information but also as structures that include attitudes and values, features of the mind which are intimately connected to but not limited by cognitive processes.

In practice it will be difficult to distinguish reliably the difference between these two types of premises, but it is not important that we be able to do so. Emotional evidence will exert pressure on the reader's entire structure of beliefs in much the same way that logical evidence will. It will provoke an accommodation of that structure to the extent that it connects with and uses as fulcra preexisting doxai that are more deeply held, more difficult to change—that is, tied to stronger emotions—than the ideas that would be changed by accepting the argument.

Rhetorical reading, then, must account for some very different sorts of claims that texts may make for their readers' belief. The reader's structure of beliefs can be pressed to change by two different types of connections between ideas: the sort that can best be described as logical—that is, generalizations that connect specific data to previously accepted ones—and less data-oriented connections that can better be described as emotional. Only if the model is extended in this way can it do justice to the complex view of the human being, not as a "thinking machine," as Weaver puts it, but as an entire being who can not only be motivated but also make judgments on the basis of values and feelings.

How Texts Persuade: The Ethical Dimension

The model of rhetorical reading as developed thus far explains persuasion in terms of connections between both logical and emotional doxai. However, it speaks of these doxai as if they were disembodied, acting on their own to demand acceptance from the reader. The epistemological viewpoint upon which this entire inquiry is premised argues that this is not the case. Invention, I have argued, is a *social* act. We develop knowledge not through an independent interaction with the facts of the universe, but in social interaction with other people. The texts that those people create are just extensions of themselves, a means to an end: the interchange of selves upon which human knowledge depends. Thus, a rhetorical model of reading must account for interactions not just between arguments but between selves.

This is Aristotle's third pistis, ethos:

> The character of the speaker is a cause of persuasion when the speech is so uttered as to make him worthy of belief; for as a rule we trust men of probity more, and more quickly, about things in general, while on points outside the realm of exact knowledge, where opinion is divided, we trust them absolutely.[29]

"Source credibility" is the nearest modern equivalent, but this rather bald term fails to convey the delicate balance of good sense, good will, and, above all, good moral character that the classical rhetoricians insisted upon.

The importance of ethos in persuasion is underlined by Booth's assertion that the rhetor—by which he means every human being capable of symbolic interaction—has a right and a duty to use her power of discourse to shape the moral and social fabric of the culture in which she lives. Particularly important to Booth's treatment of ethos is his conflation of facts and values. If what we are sharing in rhetorical interchange is not just knowledge of facts but representations of values—if we are being asked, that is, to accept as part of ourselves part of the values of those with whom we discourse—then it becomes particularly important to be able to assess not just the "message" as a disembodied argument but also its source. The character of the speaker, her honesty, wisdom, and sincerity, become particularly important "good reasons" for belief. Ethical proof, which Booth describes as "taking in by contagion," becomes a major source of evidence.

If all human beings are rhetors, however, the statement that the rhetor should be of good character is too obvious to be helpful. Of course the world would be vastly improved if we were all of good character and based all of our statements on that character; who could argue otherwise? In developing a rhetoric of reading, however, we are centrally interested in a more exact question: *How* does the reader use character as evidence for reaching a judgment on the trustworthiness of the representations of belief presented by texts?

Aristotle considered the speaker's actual character to be not directly relevant to the art of rhetoric: "This trust, however, should be created by the speech itself, and not left to depend upon an antecedent impression that the speaker is this or that kind of man."[30] Aristotle did not elaborate on the reasons for this statement, but we can assume that some combination of two factors led him to make it. First, he was describing a speaker's art, and so was naturally more interested in what the speaker must do than in "inartistic" sources of proof such as the speaker's actual character. Second, a speaker who depends on antecedent impression may not succeed with an audience who is unfamiliar with the speaker. Whether a speaker of bad character should use his art to make himself appear the opposite, Aristotle does not clearly say (though one can assume from his general concern with rhetoric as a means of defending truth that he would disapprove of such a strategy).

Later rhetoricians, particularly Quintilian and St. Augustine, insisted more strongly than did Aristotle that this impression of goodness must proceed from genuinely good character. St. Augustine, for instance, states that "the life of the speaker has greater weight in determining whether he is obediently heard than any grandness of eloquence."[31] This attitude has descended to modern rhetoricians such as Weaver, who explicitly echoes Quintilian in his declaration that "the true orator is the good man, skilled in speaking—good in his formed character and right in his ethical philosophy."[32] Yet behind even the most vehement insistence that the rhetor must actually *be* a good person lies the implication that this property is meaningless as a means of persuasion unless the audience also *perceives* the rhetor as good. The speaker who is in fact of good character must therefore use her art to "make present" (to borrow Perelman and Olbrechts-Tyteca's term) her character to the audience.

This view of ethos is particularly important for a rhetoric of reading. In applying ethos to reading, we must be able to say how the reader is able to assess the appearance of virtue in the writer. How, in short, does a writer appear through a text?

First, let us make some distinctions. There is what one might call the "inartistic" consideration of testimony, that is, judgments based on what we know of the speaker's character or of the character of the testimony in general, independent of the content of the discourse itself. Richard Whately deals with this form of evidence at some length, calling it "a kind of sign" and providing detailed discussions of how it can be weighed on the strength of factors such as number of witnesses, character of witnesses, whether the testimony is substantiated by independent witnesses, and so forth.[33] We still use such inartistic sources of evidence today, most obviously in courtroom procedure but in fact in all the dealings of our daily lives. We are clearly most apt to accept as worthy of belief statements that proceed from the greatest number of most reliable witnesses. In scholarly research, this procedure is formalized in the institution of the footnote. Statements of fact are supported by references to researchers who attest to them, and statements of opinion are supported by references to other writers who share them. The reliability of those witnesses in turn is partly substantiated by the number of citations they receive in other literature. In short, scholarly cross-referencing is simply a way of tapping into a community consensus broken down into specific representatives whose testimony is cited as evidence.

There is also a form of ethos that we might label "artistic." This is the sort of ethos in which Aristotle is most interested, that which inheres in the discourse itself. This sort of ethos is in many ways more interesting from a rhetorical point of view, because like artistic logos, it is illuminated and given life by working as an intrinsic part of a discourse under the direct command of a writer, rather than functioning externally to it. Yet, because it works invisibly, this sort of ethos is much more difficult to account for. Our impression of the author behind the work is formed by a subtle constructive process, not by the weighing of evidence that can be pointed to. In particular, the obvious problem with ethos as a feature of print conversations is that, unlike the Aristotelian rhetor, the author of a printed text is not physically present to give us an impression of his character. How can ethos affect persuasion when the author is known only through his works, and perhaps only through a single work?

To answer this question, let us first ask whether the difference between listening and reading is really as significant to the operation of ethos as the question implies. The main difference between the reader and the hearer from this perspective is the absence of delivery as a factor in persuasion. This might be a problem if ethos were conceived simply as the way a rhetor presents herself through facial expression, tone of voice, and such. However, ethos in the Aristotelian sense is not primarily an aspect of delivery. Rather, it is an aspect of invention. As one of the three pisteis, it refers to the impression the rhetor gives of herself through her choice of words and arguments, based on her solid knowledge of the virtues, the emotions, and the facts of human character. The audience of the Aristotelian orator, therefore, must construct the rhetor's character from the clues provided by the discourse in very much the same way that a reader must, for the audience of a speech has no more direct access to the interior of the person who stands before them than does the reader.

Wayne Booth confirms that it is possible—indeed inevitable—for the reader to construct a personality for the author and then to use it as a source of evidence for taking in the values of that author. In *A Rhetoric of Fiction*, Booth argues that the novelist creates an identity for himself through his writing:

> As he writes, he creates not simply an ideal, impersonal "man in general" but an implied version of "himself" that is different from the implied authors we meet in other men's works. . . . Whether we call this implied author an "official scribe," or adopt the term recently revived by Kathleen Tillotson—the author's "second self"—it is clear that the picture the reader gets of this presence is one of the author's most important effects. However impersonal he may try to be, his reader will inevitably construct a picture of the official scribe who writes in this manner—and of course that official scribe will never be neutral toward all values. Our reactions to his various commitments, secret or overt, will help to determine our response to the work.[34]

Linda Flower not only claims that readers build implied authors, but also that she has seen it happen. In "The Construction of Purpose in Writing and Reading," she reports the results of her intensive study of talk-aloud protocols collected from readers attempting to construct the meaning of texts. As well as trying to infer general aspects of the author such as intentions, "Readers would sometimes elaborate their sense of an underlying intention into a dramatic portrait of an author who thinks, believes, and does things, who has a complex web of intentions, and who succeeds or fails at realizing those intentions in the text."[35] Both the reader and the hearer, then, to a very similar degree, must construct the character of the rhetor. Each must build, from clues in the text, not only an evoked meaning but also an evoked writer, a personality that lies behind the text, and through the arguments he uses, the criteria he demonstrates, and the claims he asserts, projects a character that the reader will admire to a lesser or greater extent.

Establishing that readers *do* build images of the writer's character is only a preliminary step, however. We must go on to ask the more difficult question: *why* exactly is character persuasive—that is, why do we trust

"men of probity" more completely than others, despite the assertions of
logic that *argumentum ad hominem* is a fallacy?

Recall that the propositions that we encounter in texts are not independent of each other; they appear as *systems* of interconnected propositions. When manifested as texts we call these interconnected systems
"arguments"; conclusions are built upon sets of premises and presumed
connections between premises, many of which may be unspoken. As
with any structure, it is possible to pick apart these systems. Presented
with an argument, we may grant its conclusions but not all of its
premises, or partially grant some of the premises but organize them in
ways different from those intended by the author. (Herein lies the
creativity of human response.) But there is a natural tendency to consider
the system as a package, to admit or reject the argument as a whole.

When considered as a result of logical entailment, this tendency of
arguments to hang together is clearly a feature of logos. But logical
entailment is seldom the only, or even the major, reason for arguments
to be accepted as complete systems. Arguments are not just isolated
logical systems presented by texts. Texts are representatives of people,
and the systems of belief that readers see in texts represent samples of the
systems of belief held by the authors of those texts. These systems are not
merely logical systems but delicately balanced schematic structures that
incorporate the writer's personal experience of the world together with
the attitudes and values that provide further organizing principles. Each
system is the best estimate, of a particular human being at a particular
time, of the way the world works.

To the extent that such systems are seen as being attached to particular
human beings, they can be seen as the foundation of "character." This
ancient term can be taken to refer not just to a person's moral conduct—her
willingness to help others and to pay her income tax—but rather to the
entire system of beliefs that we perceive her to be operating under, as
manifested by tokens such as actions and words. To admire a person's
character is to admire the beliefs we perceive her as having. And if we
admire certain aspects of those beliefs, we are more likely to admire
others, not just because of an illogical "psychological transference," but
because we know from experience that beliefs are not isolated. Because
we know that such systems are complete structures, albeit not always
based purely on logical interconnections, we are encouraged to attend to
them *as* systems rather than as heaps of independent propositions, and
to accept or reject them as wholes rather than piecemeal.

Why do we bestow this sort of admiration on certain human beings
more than on others? In *A Rhetoric of Motives*, Burke answers this question
in terms of identification:

> You persuade a man only insofar as you can talk his language by speech, gesture, tonality, order, image, attitude, idea, *identifying* your ways with his. Persuasion by flattery is but a special case of persuasion in general. But flattery can safely serve as our paradigm if we systematically widen its meaning, to see behind it the conditions of identification or consubstantiality in general.[36]

Thus ethical proof depends on identifying two systems of belief, the reader's and the writer's. The power of this process is, as Burke points out, not simply dependent on flattery. For if beliefs form coherent systems, then it follows that a system congenial to ours in some respects—the respects that have already commanded admiration—is a system whose other aspects have a better chance of also being congenial—that is, of fitting into our system, rectifying its gaps, correcting its inconsistencies, answering its unanswered questions, and generally improving and extending the system of knowledge and values that is already in place.

Whereas logical and pathetic proof depends on dividing the reader's belief system into separate doxai to use as fulcra to influence others, ethos depends on the opposite movement, the impulse to treat the writer's belief systems as a whole and to accept the whole on the basis of the character of the person responsible for it. In *Modern Dogma*, Wayne Booth argues that this form of proof can often be stronger than logical proof: "We all excuse gaps in argumentative cogency if we believe that the speaker or writer is essentially reliable in sharing values we share. And it would be unreasonable not to."[37]

Because of our natural desire to maintain the coherence of our own system as economically as possible, then, we are attracted to systems associated with those who, because of our admiration for their "character" in the widest possible sense, seem to offer complementary rather than antagonistic perspectives. In extreme cases, of course, this effect can become pathological. Edwin Black notes that when a rhetor's arguments correspond with the audience's cluster of opinions, "this rhetor's word will receive increasing credit from those auditors until he becomes for them a prophet—that is, his word alone will be sufficient argument for them."[38] This explains the power of some rhetors from Joe McCarthy to Adolph Hitler to command a fanatical audience merely by feeding back, and taking credit for, the opinions the audience already holds. In this case, ethical proof short-circuits the way in which a conversation naturally modifies belief through mutual interchange, turning it instead into a self-replicating circle in which no new knowledge can be built. But this is merely a pathological extreme of the normal case. Far more often than not, our knowledge of the source of a communication provides vital evidence for the value to us of believing it.

Here, then, is a legitimate psychological reason for the transfer of acceptance from the person in general to certain of the beliefs that she presents, and thus an answer to our second question. When considered not just in the context of formal logic but in the context of naturally occurring rhetorical interaction, *argumentum ad hominem* is not necessarily as fallacious as it is sometimes made out to be. In fact, Michael Polanyi argues that scientific communities may be so isolated from each other by their epistemic vocabularies that *argumentum ad hominem* is the only source of argument available. In the absence of a common ground for other forms of persuasion, the opponent "will be made to appear as thoroughly deluded, which in the heat of the battle will easily come to imply that he was a fool, a crank, or a fraud. . . . In a clash of intellectual passions each side must inevitably attack the opponent's person."[39] Yet this collapse into ad hominem argument appears cancerous only because in this case it is not—cannot be—balanced by the other pisteis. When this balance can be maintained, our perception of the quality of the source of an argument is relevant to the acceptability of the argument, for both are part of a single system.

Different subjects of discourse will, of course, result in different grounds for admiration being more or less relevant. A person whom we admire as an excellent basketball player cannot legitimately command more respect on the subject of nuclear physics than someone whom we do not. To the extent that we translate irrelevant aspects of a person's ethos into acceptance or rejection of particular beliefs, we do indeed drift into a fallacy of relevance. But the most important aspects of ethos are generated from the most general aspects of a person's character—the Aristotelian triad of intelligence, moral character, and good will. There is no problem, except perhaps one of totally context-free formal logic, to which these aspects of personality are not at least tangentially relevant.

Ethos, then, takes its place beside pathos and logos as a source of evidence that the reader can use in deciding whether or not to accept the beliefs offered by a given set of texts. The precise balance between these three sources of evidence is necessarily dependent on many different factors: the personality of the reader, the type of text and the sort of appeals its author overtly attempts to make, and the discipline in which the transaction takes place. But as we have seen, no discipline, including the sciences, manifests a decision-making process that is completely free of all three kinds of evidence. This is a necessary result of the fact that worldviews are not isolated heaps of knowledge, but rather complex, integrated systems of logical, emotional, and ethical beliefs.

Presented schematically in this way, the rhetorical model of reading may seem to suggest that readers always choose whether or not to believe texts by deliberately applying a set of rational criteria. In particular, my use of the word "decide" suggests a conscious process. Certainly, parts of this process rise to consciousness at times; however, the simplest introspection will assure anyone that this process is most often tacit. We are only occasionally aware of all the reasons for our judgments and of all the sources of our beliefs. Reading, like other complex cognitive processes, has to be largely tacit or it simply could not work. We would not have time to evoke consciously all the factors involved in even the simplest acts of belief.

Yet, in another way, the word "decide" is apt, for it emphasizes the fact that our reactions to texts are not simple reflexes. We respond to texts according to principles that can be formulated as a model, but that does not mean that texts control us; they are not, like the sophistic rhetors that Plato satirizes, tyrants that can make us believe anything they want. Although rhetoric demands that responses be predictable to a certain extent, our complex humanity demands that we can react in ways that are not always what the author intends. Even if the process is largely tacit, we can decide whether or not to be persuaded by the beliefs that texts offer us.

The Outline of a Rhetoric of Reading

Let us look back over the model of rhetorical reading that we now have in place:

1. From a rhetorical point of view, the act of reading is a process of being persuaded to modify one's system of beliefs in order to accommodate those presented by the authors of the texts one reads. "Being persuaded" means accommodating an organized system of beliefs to take account of the new perspectives that are being offered.

2. Being persuaded begins with evoking a virtual work from a text, a virtual work that can legitimately differ from reader to reader.

3. This virtual work—loosely put, the "meaning" of the text—is evoked as a transaction between the text itself and the reader's personal repertoire of associations and knowledge, the rhetorical situation, and the shared verbal meanings collectively attached to the words of the text by the reader's linguistic community. The overarching guide in this process is the reader's attempt to impose a coherent and unified meaning on the text.

4. Being persuaded continues with a process of evaluating the meanings that one has evoked, not according to intrinsic merit as isolated entities, but according to suitability for inclusion in a system of beliefs.

5. The degree to which a system of beliefs will be accommodated to new perspectives depends on three factors:

   a. The degree to which the new perspectives logically connect with the most general, deeply held, or important ideas that make up the system already in place (logos);

   b. The degree to which the new perspectives emotionally connect with values and attitudes that contribute to the organization of the reader's belief system (pathos); and

   c. The degree to which the writer's entire structure of beliefs, attitudes and values—his "character"—is amenable to the reader's own (ethos).

6. All of these factors are highly interdependent, as are the reader's reactions to all the texts with which she is confronted. No text can be said to have "intrinsic" persuasive power even with respect to a particular reader; rather, texts fit into a system held in dynamic balance by the three modes of persuasion.

This outline of the reading process deserves the label "rhetoric" of reading not just because it employs traditional rhetorical concepts but because it treats the transaction between reader, writer, text, and situation not as a passive uptake of information but as a persuasive transaction. Reading is thus an intrinsic part of the process of rhetorical invention. It is therefore, in turn, part of a much larger movement: the building of communal knowledge through rhetorical interchange.

Notes

1. Richard C. Anderson, "The Notion of Schemata and the Educational Enterprise: General Discussion of the Conference," in *Schooling and the Acquisition of Knowledge,* ed. Richard C. Anderson, Rand J. Spiro, and William E. Montague (Hillsdale: Erlbaum, 1977), 415–31.

2. See Jean Piaget and Barbel Inhelder, *The Psychology of the Child,* trans. Helen Weaver (New York: Basic, 1969), 4–6.

3. For a useful overview of this research, see Margaret Kantz, "Toward A Pedagogically Useful Theory of Literary Reading," *Poetics, 16* (1987): 162.

4. See Gillian Brown and George Yule, *Discourse Analysis* (Cambridge: Cambridge University Press, 1983), 247.

5. Dan Sperber and Deirdre Wilson, *Relevance: Communication and Cognition* (Cambridge: Harvard University Press, 1986), 76.

6. Chaim Perelman and L. Olbrechts-Tyteca, *The New Rhetoric: A Treatise on Argumentation*, trans. John Wilkinson and Purcell Weaver (Notre Dame: University of Notre Dame Press, 1969), 4.

7. Anderson, 424.

8. Katherine Nelson, "Cognitive Development and the Acquisition of Concepts," in *Schooling and the Acquisition of Knowledge*, ed. Richard C. Anderson, Rand J. Spiro, and William E. Montague (Hillsdale: Erlbaum, 1977), 215.

9. Aristotle, *Rhetoric*, trans. Lane Cooper (Englewood Cliffs: Prentice-Hall, 1932), 8.

10. Wayne C. Booth, *Modern Dogma and the Rhetoric of Assent* (Chicago: University of Chicago Press, 1974), 144.

11. Richard M. Weaver, "Language is Sermonic," in *Language is Sermonic: Richard M. Weaver on the Nature of Rhetoric*, ed. Richard L. Johannesen, Rennard Strickland, and Ralph T. Eubanks (Baton Rouge: Louisiana State University Press, 1970), 224.

12. Aristotle, 156.

13. William M. A. Grimaldi, S. J., *Studies in the Philosophy of Aristotle's Rhetoric* (Weisbaden: Hermes, 1972), 134.

14. Aristotle, 39.

15. For surveys of the vicissitudes of logos throughout history, see Edward Corbett, "The *Topoi* Revisited," in *Rhetoric and Praxis: The Contribution of Classical Rhetoric to Practical Reasoning*, ed. Jean Dietz Moss (Washington: Catholic University of America Press, 1986), 43–58, and Elbert W. Harrington, *Rhetoric and the Scientific Method of Inquiry* (Boulder: University of Colorado Press, 1948).

16. Perelman and Olbrechts-Tyteca, 65.

17. Thomas S. Johnson, "A Comment on 'Collaborative Learning and the "Conversation of Mankind,"'"*College English, 48* (1986): 76.

18. John Trimbur, "Consensus and Difference in Collaborative Learning," *College English, 51* (1989): 602–16.

19. Kenneth Burke, *A Rhetoric of Motives* (Berkeley: University of California Press, 1950), 56.

20. Robert S. Wyer, Jr. "Attitudes, Beliefs, and Information Acquisition," in *Schooling and the Acquisition of Knowledge*, ed. Richard C. Anderson, Rand J. Spiro, and William E. Montague (Hillsdale: Erlbaum, 1977), 264.

21. Aristotle, 91.

22. Cicero, *De Oratore*, trans. E. W. Sutton and H. Rackham, vol. 1 (Cambridge: Harvard University Press, 1976), 339.

23. Nan Johnson, "Reader-Response and the *Pathos* Principle," *Rhetoric Review, 6* (1988): 157.

24. Plato, *Phaedrus*, trans. W. C. Helmbold and W. G. Rabinowitz (Indianapolis: Bobbs-Merrill, 1956), 38–39.

25. Weaver, 205.

26. Booth, 164.

27. Kenneth Burke, *A Rhetoric of Motives* (Berkeley: University of California Press, 1950), 211–12.

28. Nigel G. Gilbert and Michael Mulkay, *Opening Pandora's Box: A Sociological Analysis of Scientists' Discourse* (Cambridge: Cambridge Univ. Press, 1984), 47.

29. Aristotle, 8.

30. Aristotle, 8–9.

31. Saint Augustine, *On Christian Doctrine*, trans. D. W. Robertson (Indianapolis: Bobbs-Merrill, 1958), 164.

32. Weaver, 224.

33. Richard Whately, *Elements of Rhetoric*, ed. Douglas Ehninger (Carbondale: Southern Illinois University Press, 1963), 58–76.

34. Wayne Booth, *The Rhetoric of Fiction*, 2nd ed. (Chicago: University of Chicago Press, 1983), 70–71.

35. Linda Flower, "The Construction of Purpose in Writing and Reading," *College English, 50* (1988): 542.

36. Burke, 55.

37. Booth, *Modern Dogma*, 157.

38. Edwin Black, *Rhetorical Criticism: A Study in Method* (Madison: University of Wisconsin Press, 1978), 173–74.

39. Michael Polanyi, *Personal Knowledge: Towards a Post-Critical Philosophy* (Chicago: University of Chicago Press, 1958), 151–52.

4 The Rhetoric of Reading as a Critical Technique

Dialogic Criticism and the Unending Conversation

I have now built a complex model of rhetorical reading that sees reading as an important part of the rhetorical office of invention. The model links reading and writing as inseparable aspects of a single process: the process of building knowledge through rhetorical interchange. Now it is time to see what we might be able to do with such a model.

As I mentioned in the preface, one possible application of this model is to inform rhetorical criticism. In *Rhetorical Criticism: A Study in Method*, Edwin Black seeks to define what rhetorical criticism is, what its benefits are, and how it can most profitably be conducted.[1] Criticism in general, Black asserts, has the aim of understanding; it focuses on texts and the people who produce and receive them, not for the immediate purpose of understanding the people and events involved as such—these considerations are the proper study of the biographer, the historian, the journalist, the politician—but for the wider goal of revealing the processes that underlie the discourse. He writes, "Criticism is a discipline that, through the investigation and appraisal of the activities and products of men, seeks as its end the understanding of man himself."[2] In the case of rhetorical criticism, the activity investigated is that of persuading others; the products investigated are the texts—oral, written, or electronic—through which this activity is carried out.

I have been arguing throughout this book that the activity of persuading others is part of the larger activity of building knowledge through social interchange. The point of situating this analysis in a rhetorical context is to avoid looking at reading acts in isolation. A rhetorical analysis of reading should look at acts of reading as they occur in a larger process of epistemic interchange.

We cannot simply ask, then, how a particular person succeeds in interpreting, evaluating, and deciding whether or not to believe this or that particular text. A rhetorical analysis of reading should look at the relationship between the consumption and the production of discourse—at the way knowledge is passed on from one person to another through the paired activities of reading and writing, being continually modified as it passes from self to self. Rhetorical criticism conducted according to this model will focus not just on particular texts but on sequences of related texts by various writers. It must ask of them, not just how the writers marshall the available means of persuasion, but also how they have assembled the knowledge that they are attempting to convey—that is, how they have read as well as how they write.

This project could be conducted psychologically through a close examination of the personalities, the biographies, and the psychologies of the individual participants in the conversation. Such a study would involve close interaction with the individuals themselves as subjects of surveys, interviews, possibly interventionist data collection techniques such as think-aloud protocols, and perhaps even controlled experiments. This form of study would be valuable, for it would give us clues to the mental processes involved, clues that could not be inferred as reliably from texts alone. This is the methodology employed by researchers such as Flower and Hays, who have contributed many of the empirical insights from which I have built the present model.

However, it can also be conducted by looking only at the same data that readers must deal with every day: networks of texts severed from their living authors, embodying those authors only through the ambiguous clues that were discussed in chapter 2. When one human being wants to communicate with another, to persuade him, to modify in some way the representation of the world that he possesses, a text is often his only means of doing so. Through rhetorical criticism we can watch how these texts work as connecting strands in the rhetorical network of texts that comprises the epistemic conversation of Burke's metaphor. We can watch how ideas get passed from text to text, from reader/writer to reader/writer. We can explain elements of a text in terms of its pre-texts, the texts that contributed to its formation, as well as in terms of the writer's frame of reference, her repertoire of values and ways of seeing the world. We can watch for the ways in which writers represent in their own texts the texts of others.

This application of the rhetorical model, then, is not strictly empirical, but rather critical. The difference is that it is not an attempt to prove or disprove an empirical theory by referring to phenomena it claims to predict. Rather, it is an attempt to validate a critical model by seeing if it helps us ask and answer useful and interesting questions about the rhetorical impact of texts. In doing so, we will be attempting to observe in action the processes that have been outlined in the previous chapters: we will attempt to observe first the construction of a virtual work through the interaction of the text, the reader's repertoire, and the rhetorical situation, and second the evaluation of that work through the interaction of logical, emotional, and ethical proof.

This form of rhetorical criticism might be better termed "dialogic criticism" to distinguish it from more traditional forms of rhetorical criticism that concentrate on the persuasive strategies used by this or that rhetor. It may be thought of as a species of rhetorical criticism with a highly truncated focus on the offices of arrangement and style and a greatly expanded emphasis on the office of invention. This office is redefined to include not just the traditional methods of creating arguments but also the larger epistemic processes by which writers generate the viewpoints that will become arguments: their constructive reading and evaluation of other texts. The principal question that dialogic criticism will seek to answer, then, will be "Why do the conversants interpret and become persuaded by each other's texts in the way they do?"

Such a process will require us to speculate on the personalities, assumptions, and mindsets of the writers involved. This is of course extremely dangerous ground. It is impossible to characterize a human being *in propria persona* by examining his writings, especially a very limited sample of his writings. But this is not the aim of dialogic criticism. It is intended to establish only the assumptions and personality of the author as she appears in the text. It is therefore an attempt to reconstruct the author as she will be constructed by the other conversants in the dialogue: as a persona, an ethos that characterizes regularities in attitude that can be inferred from the text—the being that Booth labels the "implied author." Obviously, this persona is not necessarily the writer herself. However, it does represent the writer in the form that is most salient to an investigation, not of individual psychology, but rather of rhetorical interrelationships between people through texts.

This chapter will illustrate this sort of dialogic analysis by examining a series of critical analyses of James Kinneavy's *A Theory of Discourse. A Theory of Discourse*, first published in 1971, had a profound effect on the discipline of English studies. Kinneavy's goal was nothing less than to bring the paired activities of composition teaching and textual analysis out of what Kinneavy, borrowing a term from Thomas Kuhn, calls a "preparadigmatic period," a condition in which "there has not yet been erected a comprehensive system of the discipline which has received some general acceptance and which could serve as a framework for research, further speculation, innovation, even repudiation."[3] Kinneavy attempts this monumental task by synthesizing a theory of discourse from all available sources, ranging from classical rhetoric to modern rhetoric, literary theory, information theory, and language philosophy. He selects as his guiding structure the venerable communications triangle, characterizing communication as a signal linking three points:

encoder, decoder, and reality. The complex taxonomy that Kinneavy derives from this foundation is based on four categories or "aims"—expository, expressive, persuasive, and literary—according to which of the four aspects of the communications triangle is emphasized in the text. This system has not been accepted unconditionally: it has never attained the status of an encompassing paradigm for the discipline of English in the way that, for instance, Aristotle's formulations became a paradigm for traditional rhetoric. However, the complexity and detail of the taxonomic system, the depth and weight of the scholarship on which it is founded, and perhaps most importantly, the provocative possibilities for organizing a discipline that was (and to a large extent still is) having difficulty finding a structure with which to define itself, have made Kinneavy's theory a profound presence in English studies.

It is this dominating presence that makes *A Theory of Discourse* a particularly useful focus for a dialogic analysis. It has spawned a large number of other studies that argue the merits both of the book itself and of the attitude to discourse that it represents. Some of these studies have in turn spawned others that respond explicitly to the points of view articulated in earlier studies as well as to *A Theory of Discourse* itself. The intertextual web that results, then, is particularly rich in the type of dialogic relationships between texts that a rhetorical model of reading is designed to account for.

The aim of this investigation will not be to analyze *A Theory of Discourse* itself, but rather to use it as a hub that holds together a subsection of the larger conversation. The intertextual web involved embraces far more than Kinneavy's book and the analyses that mention it by name; it embraces all texts that discuss the same general topic, the taxonomizing of discourse, as well as all texts that have contributed to forming the ideas of the conversants. If I were to try to take into account all relevant texts, I would have to deal with every text that has ever touched on the subject of discourse. This example of dialogic criticism is therefore not intended to be comprehensive. Rather it is intended to highlight a limited number of texts which anchor strategic points in the dialogue and which further the goal of understanding how knowledge is built through such interactions.

These texts are those which most obviously cluster about the selected focal point: those that explicitly take a stand on the merits of *A Theory of Discourse*. Of these, I will highlight the following:

1. Jim W. Corder and Frank D'Angelo's early summaries of Kinneavy's work in the first edition of Tate's *Teaching Composition: Ten Biblio-graphic Essays*.

2. Four full-length critiques of Kinneavy, two of them positive—Timothy Crusius's articles "A Brief Plea for a Paradigm and for Kinneavy as Paradigm" and "Thinking (and Rethinking) Kinneavy"; and two negative—C. H. Knoblauch's "Intentionality in the Writing Process" and Paul Hunter's "'that we have divided / In three our kingdom.'"
3. Crusius's response to Hunter's article in the "Comment and Response" section of *College English*, and Hunter's rebuttal.

The analysis will investigate two broad classes of phenomena, in accordance with the model of reading on which it is based. First, it will look at the ways in which writers interpret source texts under the influence of the rhetorical situation and their repertoires of knowledge, assumptions, and beliefs. Second, it will examine the ways in which their judgments of these texts are influenced by the factors I have labeled logos, pathos, and ethos. It is important to understand, however, that it will not always be possible or profitable to make absolute separations between the operations of these factors. Although there is a theoretical advantage in discussing the processes of interpretation and judgment and the operation of the three pisteis as if they were separate, in practice they are inextricably intertwined. A reader is simultaneously influenced by her logical, emotional, and ethical reactions to a text, and the process of judging it affects her interpretation of it in an endlessly recursive cycle. The rhetorical model of reading will not so much allow us to separate these processes as it will remind us that at all points in our analysis we can profit by watching for ways in which these factors work in concert.

The Influence of the Rhetorical Situation

In chapter 2, I claimed that the reader's construction and evaluation of a virtual work are affected by two factors in addition to the words of the text itself: the rhetorical situation and the reader's repertoire of preexisting beliefs. The first of these two factors is particularly helpful in accounting for the differences between two of the earliest texts in the dialogue on Kinneavy: Jim W. Corder and Frank D'Angelo's chapters in Tate's collection.[4]

The rhetorical situation, as defined by Lloyd Bitzer, consists of the audience, the external constraints that govern decision (such as beliefs, documents, facts, traditions, and the like), and the exigence, the imperfection in the current state of affairs that gives rise to the need for discourse in order to set it right. In terms of the general relation between the text and the audience, the rhetorical situation of these two texts is the same; both are part of a bibliographic survey of approaches to teaching composition. This rhetorical situation involves an audience which expects a brief summary and critique of a number of the best-known texts in the field. However, the rhetorical situation also consists of a specific exigence or, as I have reinterpreted Bitzer's definition, a specific question or set of questions that a particular reader/writer is attempting to answer. Although both treatments of Kinneavy address the same general audience under the same circumstances, each does so under the influence of a different rhetorical exigence, a different set of questions. The writer's intention in writing—what he wants to tell the reader about Kinneavy's text—conditions his intention in reading Kinneavy. This difference causes each writer to evoke a different representation of Kinneavy's text.

Corder's chapter is called "Rhetorical Analyses of Writing." It is therefore not surprising that Corder focuses on the aspects of Kinneavy's scheme that are most relevant to this topic. After a brief summary of Kinneavy's four aims of discourse, Corder summarizes possible uses of Kinneavy's scheme: "This scheme of organization does not provide a rhetorical analysis. It does, however, raise a number of questions and open a number of possibilities that generate rhetorical analysis."[5] He goes on to suggest the types of questions that Kinneavy's scheme might prompt a student to ask about an essay. The view of Kinneavy's work that Corder evokes in this chapter, then, is affected by Corder's goal: identifying useful theoretical sources for rhetorical analysis.

Thus far, this analysis is hardly surprising. The effect of situation on Corder's view of Kinneavy, however, goes deeper than this rather superficial focusing of attention. Although one of Kinneavy's major innovations is the division of discourse by aim rather than by mode, Corder does not mention this aspect of *A Theory of Discourse*. Rather, he highlights another key point in Kinneavy's text, his use of the communications triangle as the foundation of his classificatory scheme. This emphasis reflects the structure of Corder's discussion as a whole: he uses *A Theory of Discourse* to illustrate a governing assumption that "a conception of rhetoric is an enabling base for rhetorical analysis."[6]

We can see this assumption illustrated in the criteria that Corder uses when he compares Kinneavy with other theorists such as Richard Ohmann and Michael Halloran. Each such comparison is based on the way the theorist in question provides a starting point for rhetorical analysis. Corder thus identifies the salient points of Kinneavy's work—the points about which he constructs his evocation of his own virtual work—with reference to the question he wishes to ask of it: how it can provide a basis for rhetorical analysis. Corder, then, does not simply analyze a constant and unchanging "text"; he analyzes a virtual work that he has evoked for himself. During the course of this evocation, his wandering viewpoint has been drawn to those parts of the text upon which the rhetorical situation has, for him, conferred presence. The virtual work that Corder has evoked is not timeless but a unique, personal "event in time," as Rosenblatt puts it, an event that represents a coming together of Kinneavy's text and a particular rhetorical context.

This does not, of course, mean that this is the only view that Corder takes or ever could take of Kinneavy's text. Because the evoked work is an event in time produced by a transient transaction between reader and text, another transaction at a different time with a different rhetorical situation will produce a different reading. However, we are interested not in all the works that Corder might evoke under the influence of Kinneavy's text, but in the particular work evoked under the influence of this particular rhetorical situation.

We can see the influence of the rhetorical situation more clearly by comparing Corder's discussion with Frank D'Angelo's chapter on "Modes of Discourse." D'Angelo's discussion shares with Corder's a generally positive tone and an attention to potential uses of the theory, as one would expect from a chapter that shares the same general rhetorical context. However, his summary and discussion of Kinneavy differs from Corder's in some revealing ways.

Throughout his book, Kinneavy insists that aims are different from modes and that *A Theory of Discourse* concerns the former.[7] Yet D'Angelo repeatedly uses the term "mode" rather than "aim." Is this really a misreading of Kinneavy, and if so, why does D'Angelo make this simple but important "error" of terminology? Perhaps D'Angelo shifts Kinneavy's terms partly as a matter of convenience; if his subject is "modes of discourse," it is certainly tidier to use the term "mode" throughout. But this symmetrical terminology reflects a deeper symmetry. D'Angelo's chapter, based on a different classification system than Corder's, compares texts not as to their usefulness as starting points for rhetorical analysis but as to the ways in which they divide forms of discourse. D'Angelo's terminology facilitates (or reflects, or creates) comparisons, not between Kinneavy and writers such as Ohmann and Halloran, but between Kinneavy and writers such as James Moffett and Alexander Bain. Moffett is the originator of a taxonomic system based on psychological distance between the reader and the writer, and Bain, a nineteenth-century compositionist, is credited with inventing the "modes" of discourse (narration, description, exposition, and argumentation); both are frequently cited as examples of writers particularly interested in categorizing discourse. By comparing Kinneavy's work with those of others who are primarily remembered for their taxonomies, D'Angelo focuses attention more on Kinneavy's categories themselves than on the communicative interactions that give rise to them.

In short, then, Corder's and D'Angelo's texts each reflects a different "virtual work" of *A Theory of Discourse*. We see these two virtual works only secondhand, of course; each is only a transient evocation in the mind of a reader, and we see them only as reflected in a text that we in turn must evoke as readers. But these second-order views—us reading Corder reading Kinneavy, and us reading D'Angelo reading Kinneavy—are enough to suggest that the differences between the virtual works is in part a result of differences between the texts with which the two readers compare that virtual work. This difference is in turn a result of the type of question the two readers wish to answer: "What are useful starting points for rhetorical analysis?" as opposed to "What are useful ways of categorizing modes of discourse?"

Here we see in action an important component of the rhetorical view of reading. The works a reader evokes are influenced not just by the words of the text but by the place of that text in the larger epistemic conversation in which the reader is immersed, a conversation that generates certain questions about the text and places it in relationship to other texts partly on the basis of those questions. Because of this influence of a broadly defined rhetorical situation, we can see that the act of reading is interpenetrated by rhetoric even when we consider only the interpretation of texts, without explicit regard to the readers' judgments of whether texts are worthy of inclusion in their own belief systems.

The Influence of Values and Assumptions

The differences between Corder's Kinneavy and D'Angelo's can be accounted for mainly by differences in rhetorical situation. When we move to later texts in the dialogue, we begin to encounter more extended texts that take a much stronger position for and against *A Theory of Discourse*. These texts make explicit some of the judgmental factors that were only implicit in Corder's and D'Angelo's analyses.

Take, for instance, Timothy W. Crusius's two articles, "A Brief Plea for a Paradigm and for Kinneavy as Paradigm" and "Thinking (and Rethinking) Kinneavy," and C. H. Knoblauch's "Intentionality in the Writing Process: A Case Study."[8] These texts all originate in a rhetorical situation somewhat different from that of Corder's and D'Angelo's texts. Corder and D'Angelo are both contributing to a survey of approaches to composition; this rhetorical situation encourages them to touch briefly on Kinneavy's work as one of many examples of composition methodology. Crusius and Knoblauch, however, are not simply surveying methodologies; they are searching for a theoretical foundation for composition teaching. This rhetorical situation leads them to take definite stands on a much more highly charged question: should the view of language and of composition teaching that underlies *A Theory of Discourse* be adopted as the paradigm for the entire discipline of composition?

As a result, these texts evidence intense and complex differences in construal and judgment. These differences can be accounted for by the ways in which *A Theory of Discourse* connects or fails to connect with these writers' preexisting values and assumptions—what classical rhetoric calls doxai. By relating the conclusions expressed in these articles to the assumptions and values that we can infer from Crusius's and Knoblauch's texts, we can account for the significant differences between the two writers' readings and judgments of Kinneavy's theories.

In "A Brief Plea," Crusius explicitly states his argument in the form of a syllogism:

(i)   As teachers of discourse, we must work from a theory of discourse—or else resign ourselves to ad hoc measures and admit that we have no systematic justification for doing anything.

(ii) While there are no complete or adequate theories of discourse at present, Kinneavy's is the most fully developed.

(iii) Therefore, we should adopt Kinneavy's theory as the paradigm for our field, thinking with his concepts, developing his categories, extending his system in principled ways, until it either becomes adequate and complete or reveals innate shortcomings that call for a new, differently conceived set of ideas.[9]

The major and minor premises of this syllogism represent the most explicit assumptions on which the conclusion is based. However, it is possible to infer more fundamental assumptions lying behind the ones that Crusius states.

Crusius's first premise, that we must work not just from theories but from a specific theory, is based on a doxa that is evident throughout the entire discussion of Kinneavy in "Plea": the responsibility of the composition theorist to reason about her discipline. Not to seek an adequate theory of discourse "amounts to an evasion of our intellectual responsibilities. . . . Our duty is to reason about discourse."[10] Such reasoning, Crusius argues, is essential to the field's "philosophical standing" and its status as an art rather than a knack.

Behind these statements we can detect not only a powerful sense of professionalism, of the need to defend rhetoric as a discipline from developments that would weaken its intellectual stance; we also can detect an intense belief in the human being as a rational animal. This belief in the responsibility and duty of the teacher to search out and pass on true propositions, combined with a faith in human rationality as the proper tool for doing so, is the habit of mind, the cluster of fundamental assumptions, that Richard Young calls "classical." Young identifies it as a faith in "the knowledge necessary for producing preconceived results by conscious, directed action."[11] With it is combined a strong desire for the sort of order that comes from synthesis. According to Crusius, its alternative, pluralism, is "too easy," too likely to slip into "facile eclecticism," too "chaotic and confusing."[12]

The values revealed here suggest not just why Crusius believes in his major premise, the need for a single paradigm, but also why he believes in his minor premise, that Kinneavy's theory is the most likely candidate for that paradigm. Kinneavy's theory is profoundly synthetic: it represents an attempt to assemble a single theory based on the insights of hundreds of authorities on rhetoric, communication, and philosophy. It is grounded in the "philosophical principles" that Crusius sees as necessary in order for a discipline to have coherence. In more practical terms, it provides the "more or less fixed notion of what constitutes adult-level performance" that satisfies Crusius's desire for teaching methods founded on rational principles rather than on mere experience and exposure.[13]

The view of reading that I have been arguing for allows us to describe this concordance of Crusius's and Kinneavy's attitudes in rhetorical terms. The heart of the enthymeme is its use of shared doxai as major premises (spoken or unspoken) that render certain propositions acceptable to the audience. In Booth's terms, these shared assumptions are some of the "warrants of assent" that induce us to take in values from the other selves with which we share the rhetorical development of knowledge. From the perspective of a productive rhetoric, the enthymeme is a device deliberately constructed by the rhetor in order to make his position acceptable. As I have redefined it from the reader's perspective, however, the enthymeme is a term that identifies the rhetorical connections that (after the fact) can be seen to have produced a rhetorical judgment. The doxa that serves this function in this case is Crusius's belief in classical approaches to knowledge and to pedagogy: a belief in order, rationality, and a unified point of view. Because Crusius perceives Kinneavy's paradigm as being constructed on these principles, he readily accepts it as a good candidate for a paradigm for composition teaching.

In Crusius's later article, "Thinking (and Rethinking) Kinneavy," we can see in more detail how the rhetorical situation and the reader's repertoire of knowledge and assumptions interact in complex and recursive ways. In this article, Crusius evidences a similar general attitude toward *A Theory of Discourse*: that Kinneavy's theory ought to be used as the base for a comprehensive paradigm of discourse. However, Crusius's repertoire of values influences not only his judgment of Kinneavy but also the very questions he sets out to ask.

Crusius admits that Kinneavy's theory as it stands is not an adequate pedagogical model because Kinneavy's abstract aims do not connect well with the ongoing experience of writing. Writers write not just to fulfill general aims but to fulfill immediate purposes: to persuade, to express, and to inform a particular somebody of a particular something in a particular context. However, Crusius defends Kinneavy's failure to distinguish aim and purpose: "In sum, on aim and purpose: Kinneavy does not distinguish them, nor should he have done so for the purpose of a general theory of discourse."[14] For Crusius, Kinneavy's theory is adequate for the purposes that Kinneavy originally intended and only needs extension to become a dynamic theory with clear pedagogical application. Crusius's guiding question thus becomes, "How exactly can we merge [aim and purpose], taking advantage of their separate contributions, while getting them to work together?"[15]

Although I have tended to treat the rhetorical situation and the writer's repertoire as two distinct factors in the evocation of a text, I have repeatedly protested that this is a theoretical convenience only; when describing a process in linear prose it is impossible to avoid giving an appearance of linearity and separateness to a process that is actually an inextricably intertwined collocation of subprocesses. Here we see how intertwined these two subprocesses really are. A vital component of the rhetorical situation, the reader's guiding questions, is itself influenced by the reader's doxai. Crusius's synthesizing mentality leads him to ask how Kinneavy's concept of aim may be combined with the concept of immediate purpose. As a result, he highlights those parts of Kinneavy's text that are most amenable to such treatment, and having found them, judges Kinneavy's theories to be in the main worthy of qualified acceptance.

The processes we have seen at work in Crusius's texts are thrown into sharp relief by comparison with another text whose author makes many of the same claims about the relation of aim and purpose but reaches diametrically opposed conclusions. In "Intentionality and the Writing Process," C. H. Knoblauch, like Crusius, points out the difference between generic "aims" as described by Kinneavy and the immediate rhetorical purpose that actually drives a given piece of discourse (what he calls "operational purpose"). However, he castigates rather than defends Kinneavy's failure to distinguish aim and purpose, and uses the pejorative term "blurring" to describe this failure. For Knoblauch, Kinneavy goes beyond failing to distinguish aim and purpose:

> Kinneavy explicitly rejects the notion of operational purpose by invoking the intentional and affective fallacies, in which the "actual" intent of a discourse is mistakenly assumed to be equivalent to the intent of its author or its impact on some intended reader. He argues that neither encoder nor decoder can reliably characterize actual intent, so that "it seems better to find the aim which is embodied in the text itself."[16]

As a result, Knoblauch does not entertain the idea that Kinneavy's theory can be adapted to serve the needs of composition pedagogy. Rather, he argues that generalized aim and operational purpose are opposite notions and that one or the other (for Knoblauch, certainly the latter) must be chosen as an operating assumption for composition pedagogy.

What is particularly interesting about these two accounts is that both writers cite a very similar kind of inductive evidence. Knoblauch's article, subtitled "A Case Study," is founded on the author's practical experience of attempting to improve the writing of business executives by helping them clarify the purpose of their texts. During this enterprise, Knoblauch reports, it was not a general aim in Kinneavy's sense but an "operational purpose" tied to the specific rhetorical context of each piece of writing that proved most helpful. Crusius admits more or less the same point, also based on teaching experience, but goes on to suggest ways in which Kinneavy's aims can be made to serve operational purpose rather than substitute for it. Thus these texts pose a particularly interesting question for dialogic criticism to answer: Why do Crusius and Knoblauch reach such different conclusions based on essentially similar inductive evidence?

The answer lies, again, in the doxai that provide the material with which the enthymemic process constructs—or in this case, fails to construct—logical, emotional, and ethical identifications between people. I have already argued that one of the most important doxai that underlies Crusius's evocation and judgment of Kinneavy is a powerful urge to synthesize. Knoblauch also admires synthesis, but he has a different notion of what it means to synthesize.

We can clarify his stand on the matter by digressing briefly to look at texts which stand outside the main line of this dialogue but which provide evidence for the doxai with which Knoblauch is operating. In *Rhetorical Traditions and the Teaching of Writing*, coauthored with Lil Brannon, Knoblauch sets strict limits on the extent to which synthesis is profitable:

> The process of merger or bringing together is not always as well-suited to intellectual progress as it is to political negotiation . . . . Intellectual consolidation is possible whenever concepts or problems can be interrelated within a single line of reasoning. But what if two lines of reasoning oppose each other, and what if evidence supporting one is stronger than evidence supporting the other?[17]

Where Crusius seeks every opportunity to synthesize, Knoblauch prefers to make distinctions and seek evidence in support of one point of view or another. In the case of Kinneavy's theories, he clearly believes that the evidence supporting an operational view of purpose is stronger than the evidence supporting a taxonomic view of aim. Consequently, he rejects the latter.

This difference about what it means to synthesize is a highly general *doxa*, a perspective on the world that would permeate any inquiry that either writer were to engage in, regardless of field. It is, in short, the sort of *doxa* that might be classed as a general *topos* ("analysis versus synthesis," perhaps). However, the two writers' views of Kinneavy's work are also affected by certain more special *topoi* that represent knowledge specific to a field of inquiry. Their respective positions on pedagogical method are examples of this sort of knowledge. Crusius suggests that general discussions of aim can help students clarify the specific purpose of a given writing project. In other words, his rationalist viewpoint (a general *topos*) informs a special *topos* specific to composition pedagogy: that students can profitably transfer knowledge from an abstract model to a particular case. This leads him to accept, if only provisionally, the knowledge offered by Kinneavy's text.

Knoblauch disagrees. In "Modern Composition Theory and the Rhetorical Tradition," an article published in the same year as "Intentionality," Knoblauch states that "no amount of theorizing about rhetoric, or grammar, or logic, or style will change writers' habits of composing as reliably as it improves their store of irrelevant precepts."[18] In *Rhetorical Traditions*, Knoblauch clarifies the difference between theory for the teacher and theory for the student:

> Teachers familiar with the abstractions can better understand the nature of composing and therefore the processes their students are striving to control. As a result, they can more surely devise classroom activities to promote growth and can more readily define their roles as facilitators of growth. But what they know about modern rhetoric only informs their teaching; it doesn't constitute class business.[19]

Thus Knoblauch sets himself in opposition to the rationalist position. He does not discount reason as an important component of the human being: the writing workshops that he and Lil Brannon recommend in later chapters of *Rhetorical Traditions* are surely examples of reasoned negotiation. However, he prefers the reason to act more or less unconsciously in a setting of collaborative social invention. For Knoblauch, direct address to the reason in the classical sense of explicit precepts is not only inadequate, but, because it focuses conscious attention on mental operations that are best conducted tacitly, actively harmful as a pedagogical tool. According to this perspective, no synthesis such as Crusius proposes is possible, for it would require bringing together two pedagogical stances that are incompatible, not complementary. Like Crusius's opinion of Kinneavy, then, Knoblauch's appears to be conditioned by a general topos (some lines of reasoning are incompatible) that interacts with a special topos specific to composition theory (the social inventional line of reasoning is preferable to the classical) to produce a judgment about a claim offered by a text. Knoblauch rejects Kinneavy's claim that his taxonomy is useful.

Here we see the operation of a primarily logical form of judgment in which a reader rejects the claims of a text because the dividing doxai outweigh any identifying doxai. However, the rhetorical model of reading reminds us that there are also emotional and ethical sources of judgment bound up with any reading act. It also reminds us that differences of judgment are partly based on different evocations of the virtual work and its implied author as well as on different evaluations of the work. These factors enter into an account of Crusius's and Knoblauch's texts, for the differences between the two accounts extend beyond a different evaluation of Kinneavy's text to a different construal of it and of Kinneavy himself. It is these construals, particularly the latter, that in this case most clearly activate the emotional and ethical aspects of judgment.

Recall that Crusius defends Kinneavy's failure to address operational purpose on the grounds that it is not germane to Kinneavy's inquiry. Knoblauch, however, portrays a Kinneavy who actively rejects rather than simply fails to emphasize operational purpose. Knoblauch's Kinneavy operates out of New Critical assumptions which Knoblauch considers obsolete. For Knoblauch, these assumptions explain Kinneavy's interest in classifying texts as isolated entities rather than in the activities performed by writers in their construction.[20] Crusius, who is not as concerned that Kinneavy neglects purpose, seeks no such explanation and does not include New Critical assumptions in his characterization of Kinneavy. If Crusius does indeed have trouble accepting New Critical assumptions, as one might expect from a writer working in an age whose critical climate is firmly post-New Critical, he does not extend that distrust to a negative construal of Kinneavy. Rather, he obviously has a profound admiration both for Kinneavy's theories and for the sort of person implied by those theories, an admiration that goes deeper than a purely logical evaluation of those theories in the abstract. The Kinneavy that he constructs—synthetic, comprehensive, philosophically grounded, and practical—fits these criteria well enough that the advantages of the theory easily outweigh the limitations that Crusius freely admits. In short, both appraisals of *A Theory of Discourse* are colored by the readers' emotional reactions to perceived character. Crusius likes the implied author of *A Theory of Discourse*. Knoblauch does not.

What we see here is not so much a direct cause-and-effect sequence as a complex interaction. It makes sense to say that Crusius and Knoblauch see Kinneavy differently because they like and dislike his theory, respectively; that is, that Knoblauch's dislike of Kinneavy's conclusions gives greater presence to the aspects of the author that Knoblauch finds negative, thereby increasing the support for Knoblauch's judgment and helping to keep his view of Kinneavy consistent and coherent. However, it makes equal sense to say the opposite: that Crusius's and Knoblauch's judgment of Kinneavy's theories do not just give rise to but are also supported by their emotional and ethical reactions to an implied author who appears to one reader as a tremendous synthetic intelligence and to the other as a scholar who has been duped by his outworn New Critical perspectives. The processes of construal and judgment, of logos, pathos, and ethos, are not separable. We cannot say with confidence which aspects of Crusius's and Knoblauch's judgments are logical and which emotional, which are reactions to Kinneavy's theory and which to the character of the author they construct. Nor are these processes linear. Rather, they are recursive, all working in concert as part of a complex enthymemic process which results in different readers' arriving at highly varied conclusions about the same text.

Of course, we could also examine the reasons for these doxai themselves; that is, we could ask why Crusius appears to be more classical and Knoblauch more New Romantic, why Crusius seeks to synthesize and Knoblauch to distinguish points of view. These fundamental assumptions must, like all aspects of a reader's repertoire, be conditioned by a combination of life experience and rhetorical input. Like the conversation of humanity itself, dialogic criticism can be complex to the point of infinite regress. The decision as to where to stop such an analysis must be made not on theoretical but on rhetorical grounds: one stops when one's account is satisfactory for the purpose intended. For the purpose intended here—illustrating the ways in which dialogic criticism can account for rhetorical interrelationships between texts—we need not peel any more layers off these two rather abused onions.

Ethos and Pathos: A Closer Look

Though all of the reading processes that I have identified will function to some extent in all texts, it often happens that one or another of them will be especially highlighted in a particular text. A case in point is Paul Hunter's article "'that we have divided / In three our Kingdom': The Communication Triangle and *A Theory of Discourse*."[21] This text is particularly interesting for the way in which Hunter extends his appraisal of Kinneavy's work to a highly conscious and deliberate attempt to characterize Kinneavy as a person. In doing so, he not only foregrounds ethos, a mode of judgment that was more in the background in the work of Crusius and Knoblauch, but also highlights pathos as a mode of judgment through the way he reveals emotional responses to the values implicit in the Kinneavy he evokes.

Hunter begins by announcing that he will criticize Kinneavy's theory primarily on the grounds that its basis, the communication triangle, is more appropriate to speaking-listening than to writing-reading processes.[22] This is the sort of argument that we might characterize as an argument from logos. However, a large portion of the article in fact comes to be dominated by a line of argument that Hunter calls "ancillary": the argument that Kinneavy's theory, and by extension Kinneavy himself, is "essentially moralist."[23] This argument involves a construction of Kinneavy's character—not of his personal character in the sense of whether he parks illegally or avoids paying his taxes, but rather in the sense of what we might call his "textual character," the sum of the theories he espouses and the underlying attitudes and values implied by those theories.

In his response to Crusius's comment on "'that we have divided'" (to be dealt with in more detail later in this chapter), Hunter recognizes this distinction himself: "My complaint is with the text, not with the scholar who wrote it . . . [It] should not be read as an attack on the man, one of the most helpful and influential teachers of my undergraduate years."[24] Hunter's view of Kinneavy "the man," that is, Kinneavy as known from personal acquaintance, satisfies the traditional definition of positive ethos: Kinneavy appears as a person of intelligence and good will, well suited to be a colleague and mentor. However, for the purpose of deciding whether to accept or reject a theoretical perspective, the more important ethos is that of the textual Kinneavy, who emerges, for Hunter, as a moralizing, intolerant positivist. This distinction underlines Aristotle's point that the ethos projected by the speech is more important to the reception of the speech than any impression of character gained from prior acquaintance.

Like Knoblauch, Hunter finds Kinneavy deeply entrenched in New Critical assumptions, and opens his article with an assertion to that effect. However, he goes on to probe below the New Critical attitude to discourse and expose what he sees as the underlying reason for Kinneavy's attraction to New Critical perspectives: a belief in scientific objectivity and a positivistic attitude toward truth. For instance, Hunter traces Kinneavy's distrust of persuasive rhetoric to this positivistic outlook: "What we see in Kinneavy's examples . . . is the type of interpretation of texts produced by one who believes that logic and rhetoric are fundamentally at odds: logic concerned with truth, rhetoric concerned with manipulation."[25] Because of Kinneavy's tendency to see the world in terms of this dichotomy—a dichotomy that Kinneavy, Hunter argues, treats as an objective fact—Kinneavy insists on devaluing persuasive communication and privileging scientific discourse.

In the second section of the article, the effect of ethos is further deepened and blended with a form of judgment by pathos, seen in Hunter's emotive reaction both to Kinneavy's theories themselves and to his textual character. From characterizing Kinneavy's theories as "positivistic" and "scientific," Hunter progresses to more pejorative terminology. He accuses Kinneavy not just of monism but of an "*intolerant monism*" (my emphasis), which he contrasts with an "authentic pluralism."[26] Hunter's main evidence is Kinneavy's remark that those who espouse forms of artistic interpretation other than the one he labels "objective" are prostituting art. From this remark and from Kinneavy's suggestion that people can be categorized by their ways of thinking, Hunter infers that Kinneavy betrays an "implicit categorization of people along the lines of Plato's *Republic*."[27] This tendency to categorize, combined with what Hunter sees as his "positivistic" belief in a single objective truth rather than a relativistic or pluralistic stance, "could lead to a perpetuation—even to a justification—of social stereotyping."[28] This is a stance that, for Hunter, "is not a cure; it is poison."[29]

In traditional rhetorical criticism, Hunter's increasing swing to heavily emotional terms such as "intolerant" and "poison" could be identified as an important persuasive strategy. Writing as though he were an advocate for the prosecution, Hunter associates the accused with qualities that he knows his audience (liberal, educated Americans) will consider base, reinforced with emotional terms such as "poison." His use of this strategy is particularly explicit when, after characterizing Kinneavy as guilty of social stereotyping, he asks "how closely we as teachers of writing want to be identified with that."[30] Clearly he is not only recognizing the doxai of his audience—a deeply ingrained distrust of intolerance and stereotyping—but also using the American emotional response to racial discrimination by tangentially associating his opponent with this ultimate badge of ignoble character. Thus he is using pathos as an important mode of rhetorical proof.

However, a dialogic analysis founded on a rhetorical model of reading suggests that there is more to this matter. Through this lens, these strategies appear not only as Hunter's attempts to persuade his readers, but also as evidence for the ways in which Hunter himself has been persuaded. Pathos becomes a mode of judgment as well as mode of proof. In this case, pathos is inseparably wedded to ethos, for Hunter's emotional reaction is not just to Kinneavy's theories but to Kinneavy himself. Clearly he sees Kinneavy's theoretical stance not as a set of separate theories but as an interdependent structure of beliefs that forms a coherent whole. He is thus encouraged not only to consider some of Kinneavy's ideas as being predictable from others, but also to extrapolate from the beliefs that are manifest in the text to others which are not. As a result, Hunter uses Kinneavy's expressed ideas on discourse analysis as a basis for inferring a wider aspect of character, a tendency toward social stereotyping. Ultimately, Hunter rejects Kinneavy's entire structure of beliefs on the basis of its incompatibility, both logical and emotional, with doxai that Hunter holds with particularly deep conviction.

Thus Hunter's article not only shows us *that* pathos is an important factor in judgment, but also adds to our understanding of *how* it functions. Terms such as "monism," "moralizing," and "stereotyping" (negative) and "pluralism" (positive), according to the rhetorical model of reading, are not merely persuasive devices, though they certainly are that as well. They are also important mechanisms of pathetic judgment. They are "terministic screens," in Kenneth Burke's sense, terminologies that direct the attention in certain ways rather than others, that encapsulate certain attitudes to reality—that are, in short, indispensable tools with which to think and to feel.[31] In Hunter's text, we can see how Hunter teases out the assumptions that he feels underlie Kinneavy's approach to discourse, resolves them into a few key terms, and tests them by considering the values attached to those terms. It is because the values he attaches to "monism," "stereotyping," and "moralizing" are all negative that he finds Kinneavy's theory of discourse wanting.

This business of encapsulating values in key terms, of course, can be a facile means of avoiding thought. Richard Weaver, for instance, points out the danger of idly tossing around "god terms" and "devil terms" in order to provoke a knee-jerk reaction from audiences who blindly attach powerful positive and negative values to labels.[32] However, just as Booth insists that there are both good and bad reasons for judgment, so there are god and devil terms which are philosophically grounded and ones that are perverse or sinister. The trick in using terms properly, according to Weaver, is not to avoid rhetorically loaded terms but to make sure that they are rhetorically loaded in some rational and justifiable manner. If one's terms and the emotional response that one attaches to them are truly thoughtful, grounded in a dialectical attempt to apprehend reality and not just to concur with what is going on around one, then they can be the tools of genuine rhetorical inquiry. They can be a means of seeking what Booth would call "good reasons" for holding a theory by testing it not just against "reality" but also against the values implicit in it. Key terms such as these, then, are important to the pathetic mode of judgment because of the ways in which they can summarize and juxtapose for comparison entire clusters of emotional attitudes.

These four texts, then, reveal how writers' beliefs and values, their *doxai*, operate as part of an intertwined rational, emotional, and ethical system of judgment. Hunter's evaluation of Kinneavy, from the perspective of rhetorical reading, is not simply a logical judgment. Like the evaluations of Crusius and Knoblauch, it proceeds from an ethical view of a human being and his theories as a bundle of attitudes, attitudes which can be deduced from his texts and compared with one's own, emotionally as well as rationally, to produce good reasons for judgment. It is, then, at least in part an *argumentum ad hominem*, a logical fallacy, but it is not a rhetorical fallacy. The source of an argument is a vital part of a rhetorical decision to accept or reject a thesis presented for our assent.

Further Turns in the Conversation: Responses and Rebuttals

Thus far this inquiry has been limited to a comparative analysis of rhetorical reading; that is, I have been comparing various responses to Kinneavy's text as if they were largely independent of each other. However, one of the most important features of the conversational model of rhetorical interchange is that it draws attention to the ways in which texts form networks of interconnections. To return to Burke's metaphor of the unending conversation, each conversant does not simply stand up, say her piece on the subject at hand, and then sit down. The conversation ranges back and forth: "Someone answers; you answer him; another comes to your defense; another aligns himself against you, to either the embarrassment or gratification of your opponent, depending upon the quality of your ally's assistance."[33] Applied to the dialogue under investigation here, this conversational model predicts that each of Kinneavy's critics will be influenced not just by Kinneavy's text but by countless other texts, in the forefront of which will naturally be other critiques of Kinneavy. If we wish to explore the implications of the rhetorical model of reading to the fullest extent possible, then, we must go on to use it to account for the ways in which the participants in a multiparty conversation judge not only Kinneavy's text but also each other's.

Within the texts already cited there is some evidence of such interrelationships. Hunter, for instance, explicitly uses a refutation of Crusius's position as a take-off point: "I reject Timothy Crusius's proposition that 'we should adopt Kinneavy's theory as the paradigm for our field' as a dangerous and reactionary suggestion."[34] But such direct evidence of intertextual influence among the participants of this particular dialogue is somewhat rare. It is more common for writers to refer to other writers who have proposed taxonomic schemes similar to Kinneavy's. Crusius, for instance, relates Kinneavy's taxonomy to those of Aristotle, Burke, and Young, Becker, and Pike; Knoblauch cites those of Richard Lloyd-Jones, James Britton, and James Moffett. In short, they tend to cite sources that are parallel to *A Theory of Discourse* rather than to their own critiques of it.

This is reasonable in view of the fact that Kinneavy's theory itself holds more inherent interest to these writers than do other critiques of it. When one's rhetorical purpose is to comment on taxonomies of discourse, it is reasonable to cite taxonomies of discourse rather than rival critiques. For dialogic criticism, however, the conversation becomes more interesting at a later stage when the participants begin specifically replying to each other's work. At this point, as writers attack each other's viewpoints and defend their own, when "someone answers; you answer him; another comes to your defense," we begin to see more clearly how their perspectives differ and how they have been influenced by how they have read each other's texts as well as by how they have read Kinneavy's.

The later part of the dialogue between Hunter and Crusius takes place in the "Comment and Response" section of *College English*. This section gives writers an opportunity to reply directly to specific articles in the journal and gives the writers of the original articles an opportunity for further rebuttal. These sequences provide a particularly explicit view of the ways in which writers read each other's texts. In the case of the dialogue on Kinneavy, the writers whose reading is displayed in this way are Timothy Crusius and Paul Hunter.

Crusius's reply to Hunter is occasioned by Hunter's claim that Crusius's proposal is "a dangerous and reactionary suggestion." His reply underlines many of the points that have been noted already, for he defends his attraction to Kinneavy's theories by restating and expanding on many of the arguments already made in "Plea" and "Thinking."

Though Crusius has modified the highly positive view of Kinneavy demonstrated in "Plea" by the time he writes his comment on Hunter, he has not modified his belief in synthesis: "My position now is that Kinneavy makes the single greatest contribution to a *synthesis* of theories better than Kinneavy alone, or Moffett alone, and so forth."[35] In his response to Crusius, Hunter, in turn, clarifies and expands his earlier argument that the communications triangle is an inadequate basis for a theory of writing. In general, we see the familiar pattern of competing but internally coherent structures of belief. Crusius, backed by authorities such as Ong and Moffett, states the traditional view that literacy is based in orality, while Hunter, backed by poststructuralist authorities such as Foucault, Ricoeur, Bloom, and Derrida, reiterates his earlier argument that writing should *not* be taught as an extension of speech.

These later texts in the dialogue demonstrate how an evocation of a work and its implied author—an "event in time" rather than a stable entity—can shift under the influence of other texts. Though neither alters his basic position on Kinneavy, each writer is stimulated by other critics of Kinneavy, including each other, to create a new evocation of Kinneavy and a new perspective on his theories. This re-evocation further illustrates the interaction between repertoire and rhetorical situation. An important manifestation of the rhetorical situation is the set of questions that a reader asks of a text. However, these questions are, of course, influenced by other aspects of the rhetorical situation, which is the sum total of all the components of the reading transaction: the reader, her purpose, the writer, his purpose, and the physical circumstances surrounding the composition and comprehension of the text. The prior texts in the conversation are clearly part of this situation. By creating the need to answer and to come to others' and one's own defense, these texts have a profound influence on the way readers interrogate the original text (in this case, *A Theory of Discourse*). They are also part of each reader's repertoire of personal experience. In both respects, then, the prior texts influence the way each reader creates a new evocation of each text in the conversation—his own, the other critics', and Kinneavy's itself—as well as a new evocation of all the implied authors in the dialogue. Since a virtual work is an event in time, a new time will bring about a new event.

The criticisms of people such as Hunter create a rhetorical situation that leads Crusius to undertake what is essentially a piece of dialogic criticism himself: he wishes to account for the resistance that many critics, Hunter included, feel toward Kinneavy's theories. Thus, he constructs a new evocation of Kinneavy, this time from a new point of view and for a new purpose: not to improve his own representation of the world by apprehending Kinneavy's, but to help him understand the reaction to Kinneavy of other critics. To account for this reaction, Crusius evokes a Kinneavy whose textual character contains contradictions. This Kinneavy is influenced both by semiotics, which Crusius describes as "ahistorical and universalistic," and by traditional rhetoric, which "pulls him toward the relatively concrete domain of temporal process."[36] The result is a theory that inevitably pulls in contradictory directions—toward impossibly general questions answered by relatively context-specific examples. "No wonder," comments Crusius, "we feel somewhat ill at ease."

Yet Crusius maintains his original position that the inadequacies in Kinneavy's theory are not insurmountable. By identifying for himself more clearly the problems generated by the structuralist side of Kinneavy's theory, he clarifies for himself the remedy: to refuse to reify the aims in the ways that a structuralist perspective (he claims) can lead one to do, and instead to treat the aims only as heuristic constructs that can help us "get on with the task of articulating the conventions of discourse that we are asking our students to write."[37] Crusius, therefore, has not been moved to accommodate his structure of beliefs to arguments such as Hunter's which are diametrically opposed to it. Those opposed arguments, however, have had their effect. They have encouraged Crusius to re-evoke Kinneavy in a way that reshapes and modifies his response to *A Theory of Discourse*. He has been persuaded to be more aware of the dangers of reification and of the internal contradictions within Kinneavy's theory.

Thus we see again the complexity of rhetorical inquiry. One participant does not necessarily bring another to believe as she does, but the enmeshing of ideas in a complex set of interchanges contributes to the growth of individual knowledge—in Booth's terms, to the making of the self through the taking in of other selves. Because the rhetorical situation continually shifts when new texts and new perspectives join the conversation, each conversant is continually forced to re-evoke her view of other texts and of the reality they attempt to represent.

A Theory of Discourse itself is not the only text, and Kinneavy not the only author, that is evoked and re-evoked in this phase of the dialogue. In responding directly to Hunter's criticisms of Kinneavy, Crusius also evokes a representation of Hunter, an evocation crucial to the way Crusius both understands and judges Hunter's arguments. Crusius seeks to understand what he sees as Hunter's main charge against Kinneavy, the charge that Kinneavy is moralist rather than pluralist. To do so he constructs for himself and his readers the values that he sees Hunter attaching to key terms in the argument:

> Does Kinneavy's theory lead us away from "genuine pluralism"? We
> might ask first, What must pluralism be to be genuine? Hunter seems

> to believe that pluralism and a sense of what is right, suitable,
> appropriate (i.e., "moralism"?) are somehow at odds. Apparently for
> him a genuine pluralism must be open to everything, making no
> discriminations about relative value.[38]

For a rhetoric of production we can see this passage as rhetorical strategy: the strategy of reiterating your opponent's stand in terms that make it easy to refute (a strategy that, when taken to excess, becomes the dishonest "straw man" technique). But through the lens of a rhetoric of consumption, it also appears as a reflection of Crusius's attempt to understand Hunter, to create a "textual character" for him in order to facilitate a judgment.

What Crusius finds at the bottom of Hunter's argument is a dichotomy between moralizing on the one hand and pluralism on the other, a dichotomy that Crusius finds unacceptable and which causes him to reject Hunter's argument. However, simply rejecting Hunter's argument is not satisfactory. In order to maintain the coherent structure of his own beliefs as well as to convince his audience, Crusius must find a satisfactory alternative to this dichotomy. To do so, he rearranges the terms of Hunter's argument to accentuate the values that he wishes to maintain. He relabels the attitude that Hunter calls "moralizing" with less negative terms such as "hierarchy of values," thus justifying his acceptance of Kinneavy's attitude. He reanalyzes the term "pluralistic" into two terms: "eclecticism," which he associates with Hunter's values, and "genuine pluralism," which he associates with Kinneavy's. Here the division of "pluralism" into two concepts allows Crusius to remove the incompatibility arising from Hunter's opposition of "pluralism" and "moralizing." This allows him to reject the concept of eclecticism while embracing a counterpart that is compatible with having a "hierarchy of values."

Here we see the principle of consistency-building fulfilled in practice. Recall that comprehension involves an assumption that the text provides an internally coherent representation of the world. In turn, the reader also wishes to maintain the consistency of his own representation of the world. As a result, the enthymemic process becomes highly recursive. A reader will be more likely to accept the propositions offered by a text if they are consistent with his own doxai. Reciprocally, a desire to accept certain propositions presented by a text provides a motivation to evoke the work in ways that remove inconsistencies both within the work and between the work and the reader's own repertoire of doxai. To do otherwise would be to admit into one's own system of beliefs a set of perspectives that would degrade rather than enhance its coherence.

As I have said, this process, when taken to an extreme, is simply a matter of seeing what one wishes to see, of justifying a prejudgment of a text by interpreting it in the most favorable manner possible. But as with all other components of a rhetoric of reading, justifying a prejudgment is only an extreme version of an act that is an inevitable and positive part of a recursive process: judging on the basis of an evocation and evoking on the basis of a judgment. In this particular case, the re-evocation is motivated by another text (Hunter's), which gives presence to the potential inconsistencies which Crusius must remove.

Hunter, for his part, undertakes a similar evocation of Crusius, for the same reasons: to understand and judge Crusius's arguments. The way Hunter evokes Crusius emphasizes the gulf between them. "I wonder," ponders Hunter, "if Crusius realizes how great the differences are between his language theory and my own."[39] This difference turns on a basic disagreement over the relationship between oral and written communication. Crusius, like the structuralist linguists, sees writing as derived from speech. This view makes it reasonable to derive a theory of writing from the speech-oriented communication triangle. Hunter on the other hand sees the relationship from the poststructuralist perspective which holds that the processes are not hierarchically related. It is this difference which lies at the foundation of his argument against a theory of writing based on the oral communication triangle. In his response to Crusius, Hunter is forced to make this point more explicit than he did in "'that we have divided.'" Moreover, he condenses the differences between himself and Hunter to another pair of opposed terms, "structuralism" versus "poststructuralism."[40] By associating Crusius with structuralism (an association that Crusius himself never makes), Hunter builds an impression of Crusius's textual character that is incompatible with Hunter's poststructuralist beliefs.

Here we see the circle of evocation and judgment working in the opposite direction, in the service of division rather than identification. To maintain the consistency of his own belief system, Hunter must either fend off Crusius's attempts to convince him of a different system or reorganize his own system completely. We have already noted how the operation of logos depends on connecting new perspectives with old ones, a technique that Burke refers to as using some of the audience's beliefs to support a fulcrum by which other beliefs will be changed. To effect such a sweeping change in Hunter's belief system, Crusius would have to find a fulcrum of argument, a portion of Hunter's belief system with which he could identify the propositions that he wishes to promote and which is more deeply rooted than the ones he wishes to change. The strategy fails because Hunter, motivated by his desire to maintain the consistency of his own belief system, succeeds in evoking Crusius's argument in ways that make it easy to resist. By using the familiar strategy of manipulating key terms, Hunter severs rather than builds enthymemic identifications between Crusius and himself.

In sum, though neither has been significantly moved from his original position, Crusius and Hunter emerge from the exchange having understood Kinneavy's system and their own reactions to it from new perspectives. By evoking each other's positions, accepting parts and refuting others for the benefit of a third-party audience (the readers of *College English* and by extension all the other members of their discipline), Crusius and Hunter have not only reformed and deepened their own reactions to Kinneavy but have advanced a dialogue that started with the first reviews and summaries of Kinneavy such as Corder's and D'Angelo's, a dialogue that is part of a larger conversation about discourse theory that started with Kinneavy's classical sources. Thus we see the power of rhetorical reading to build and rebuild knowledge, not just incrementally, by adding new pieces to an existing structure, but by continually provoking a reassessment of the old structure and its components.

In turn, this dialogue illustrates the power of the rhetorical model of reading as a critical tool. The arguments that the conversants choose, the strategic manipulations of terminology they engage in, and the dichotomies they choose to accept or reject, are accounted for in the dialogic model as part of a process of reexamining and testing knowledge systems through social interchange. By examining their texts from this perspective, we catch the writers in the Boothian act of making themselves by taking in other selves.

Conducted in this manner, a dialogic form of rhetorical criticism fulfills Black's program for rhetorical criticism. By enabling a precise account of rhetorical interactions, it promotes a more general understanding of human beings and the way they create knowledge through discourse. This explanatory power of dialogic criticism does not lie just in the labels that it allows us to attach to features of the exchange. Rather, it lies in the power of those labels and the general model of epistemic rhetoric that backs them to draw certain features of texts to our attention. The terministic screens created by this model of reading direct our attention to evidence that the writers are not simply trying to persuade others of a predetermined point of view, but rather are creating their own representation of the world by looking for connections between their own repertoire of beliefs and those they perceive in their sources.

Notes

1. Edwin Black, *Rhetorical Criticism: A Study in Method* (Madison: University of Wisconsin Press, 1978). It should be noted that one of Black's major theses in *Rhetorical Criticism* is that neo-Aristotelian criticism is a limited and largely obsolete methodology and must be superseded (see especially p. 131). Because so much use is made here of Aristotle's pisteis and his theory of the enthymeme, it is important to point out that Black's work is being used as a classic statement of the *goals* of rhetorical criticism, but not necessarily of its *methods*. There is a good deal of wisdom in Black's work, but his rejection of Aristotle is fundamentally at odds with the stance adopted here.

2. Black, 9.

3. James A. Kinneavy, *A Theory of Discourse: The Aims of Discourse* (New York: Norton, 1971), 2.

4. Jim W. Corder, "Rhetorical Analysis of Writing," in *Teaching Composition: Ten Bibliographical Essays*, ed. Gary Tate (Fort Worth: Texas Christian University Press, 1976), 223–39; and Frank J. D'Angelo, "Modes of Discourse," in Tate, 111–35.

5. Corder, 227.

6. Corder, 226.

7. See especially Kinneavy, 38.

8. Timothy W. Crusius, "A Brief Plea for a Paradigm and for Kinneavy as Paradigm," *Freshman English News*, 12.3 (1983): 1–3; Timothy W. Crusius, "Thinking (and Rethinking) Kinneavy," *Rhetoric Review*, 3 (1985): 120–30; C. H. Knoblauch, "Intentionality in the Writing Process: A Case Study," *College Composition and Communication*, 31 (1980): 153–59.

9. Crusius, "Brief Plea," 1.

10. Crusius, "Brief Plea," 1.

11. Richard Young, "Arts, Crafts, Gifts and Knacks: Some Disharmonies in the New Rhetoric," in *Reinventing the Rhetorical Tradition*, ed. Aviva Freedman and Ian Pringle (Ottawa: Canadian Council of Teachers of English, 1980), 56.

12. Crusius, "Brief Plea," 1–2.

13. Crusius, "Brief Plea," 2.

14. Crusius, "Thinking," 124.

15. Crusius, "Thinking," 125.

16. Knoblauch, 155.

17. C. H. Knoblauch and Lil Brannon, *Rhetorical Traditions and the Teaching of Writing* (Upper Montclair: Boynton/Cook, 1984), 17.

18. C. H. Knoblauch, "Modern Composition Theory and the Rhetorical Tradition," *Freshman English News*, 9.2 (1980): 3.

19. Knoblauch and Brannon, 102.

20. Knoblauch, "Intentionality," 154–55.

21. Paul Hunter, "'that we have divided / In three our kingdom': The Communication Triangle and *A Theory of Discourse*," *College English*, 48 (1986): 279–87.

22. Hunter, 280.

23. Hunter, 280.

24. Paul Hunter, "Paul Hunter Responds [to Timothy W. Crusius]," *College English*, 49 (1987): 221.

25. Hunter, "Divided," 281.

26. Hunter, "Divided," 283.

27. Hunter, "Divided," 286.

28. Hunter, "Divided," 286.

29. Hunter, "Divided," 286.

30. Hunter, "Divided," 283.

31. See Kenneth Burke's essay "Terministic Screens" in *Language as Symbolic Action* (Berkeley: University of California Press, 1966), 44–62.

32. Richard Weaver, "Ultimate Terms in Contemporary Rhetoric,"in *Language is Sermonic: Richard M. Weaver on the Nature of Rhetoric*, ed. Richard L. Johannesen, Rennard Strickland, and Ralph T. Eubanks (Baton Rouge: Louisiana State University Press, 1970), 87–112.

33. Kenneth Burke, *The Philosophy of Literary Form: Studies in Symbolic Action* (Berkeley: University of California Press, 1941), 110–11.

34. Hunter, "Divided," 280.

35. Timothy Crusius, "A Comment on '"that we have divided / In three our Kingdom": The Communication Triangle and *A Theory of Discourse*,'" *College English*, 49 (1987): 214.

36. Crusius, "Comment," 216.

37. Crusius, "Comment," 217.

38. Crusius, "Comment," 218.

39. Hunter, "Responds," 220.

40. Hunter, "Responds," 220.

5 Implications for Teaching and for the Art of Rhetoric

Teaching Research Writing: The Knack and the Art

In the preface to this book, I claim that an understanding of the rhetorical nature of reading can help us to teach the art of research, an art that is central to the entire academic community and, as performed in a less formal way, to the entire process of living. Here, I wish to make good on the implied promise to explain how this is so. But first, I believe that it is important to address the question of why research-based writing as such should be taught in the first place.

Richard Larson, among many others, has argued that there is really no such thing as a separate genre called "the research paper." While research can inform almost any type of writing, Larson argues, research

> is itself the subject—the substance—of no distinctly identifiable kind of writing. . . . There is nothing of substance or content that differentiates one paper that draws on data from outside the author's own self from another such paper.[1]

Larson's point is well taken. Among the other oddities of the composition class, perhaps the supreme oddity is that it is only here that research, the universal ether that interpenetrates all formal inquiry, becomes "the research paper," a separate genre that occupies a separate little section of the course. The success of writing-across-the-curriculum (WAC) programs argues strongly that "research writing" must be let out of its cell in the composition classroom and taught throughout the academic continuum.

Yet it is still a fact of life in the disciplinized academic world that teaching research and teaching writing somehow drift apart. Teachers in other disciplines expect students to write papers based on research, but often do not understand or care how to teach students to do it. Many a well-intentioned WAC program has foundered on this rock. Composition teachers also attempt to teach research-based writing—Ford and Perry reported in 1982 that 84 percent of freshman composition classes included a research writing component[2]—but we, too, seem to know little about what we are doing. The available literature on teaching the research paper provides some useful insights, but it tends to offer mostly

102

scattered suggestions for ways of teaching specific and often superficial aspects of the research paper: how to use 3 x 5 cards more effectively, how to find more stimulating topics, how to eliminate plagiarism. In his survey of the state of the art, Ford sums up the situation thus:

> There are exceedingly few articles of a theoretical nature or that are based on research, and almost none cites even one other work on the subject. They are not cumulative. Rather, the majority are of the short, often repetitive, show-and-tell variety characteristic of an immature field.[3]

The problem is not that work on the pedagogy of research is inherently of poor quality. It is that, despite the rapid maturing of composition theory in general and the rediscovery of its roots in the rhetorical tradition, this particular branch of composition theory is still, as Ford suggests, an immature field. And one of the most telling marks of an immature field is that it does not yet have a clear view of what it is that it is attempting to do. In the *Gorgias*, Plato castigates sophistic rhetoric for being a "knack" rather than an "art." Its practitioners, he charges, know by trial and error how to achieve certain effects, but they have no real understanding of what they are teaching and therefore can impart no real knowledge. Composition teachers are in precisely this position: we do not have an encompassing definition of what it really means to compose discourse based on other people's texts. What does it really mean to search, not just through one's own storehouse of knowledge and values, but through other writers' storehouses, in search of the answer to a question? What does it mean to interpret large numbers of often-conflicting texts, evaluate the opinions expressed, and create from an amalgam of one's own and other people's beliefs a new answer, a new piece of knowledge that is not just a patchwork of sources but an original system of beliefs that could not have existed without the believer's having considered other texts? Without a model of rhetorical reading to inform it, the teaching of reading and writing in general, and particularly of the intensely dialogic form of the research paper, will be no more than a knack: a "show-and-tell" skill, to use Ford's term again, rather than a discipline grounded in knowledge. When it does get results, those results will not be repeatable because we will not know how we really achieved them.

Whether writing based on research is taught across the disciplines or in a little corner of the composition class, I believe that it falls to us as rhetorical theorists and practitioners to develop an understanding both of what this process is and of how to teach it—to turn the knack into an art. The model of rhetorical reading that I have outlined is intended partly as a prerequisite for this task of developing a philosophically grounded pedagogy of research-based writing.

What to Teach

The first step in turning a knack into an art is to be able to describe fully what one is trying to produce. The rhetorical model of reading provides an account of mature performance in the activity of reading for knowledge. This implies not just a descriptive account of what typically *is done* by good readers, but also a normative account of what students must *be able to learn to do* in order to become good readers. It implies, that is, a list of attributes and skills that our students should ideally be able to attain.

First, the model implies that successful readers have a richly stocked repertoire of prior knowledge. The schemata in which this knowledge is stored both help readers construct interpretations of texts and help them judge which interpretations are worth believing. Because it bases the judgmental process on the model of the enthymeme, on connections between the reader's doxai and those that inform the writer's conclusions, the model suggests that readers must be able to access not only their own repertoires but also those of others. That is, it suggests that they must be able to infer the patterns of assumptions that have led other writers to their conclusions. Like the participants in the dialogue on Kinneavy, good readers construct each other.

The rhetorical model of reading also implies that good readers have learned how far they can trust not only their strictly logical analysis of a work as a set of propositions, but also their emotional responses to the values underlying those propositions and their ethical responses to the implied character of the writer. A filmy, shifting image of a human being can emerge from behind even the driest and most "objective" text, and we can decide whether or not we like that person and her ideas. This decision, though not based strictly on logic or "the facts," can still be one of a constellation of good reasons for accepting or rejecting a set of beliefs.

A common image of the research process, that it is simply a means of acquiring data, does not encourage teachers to teach these skills of active construction and evaluation. This view tends to be conveyed more by omission than by positive statement. Almost all composition textbooks contain a section on writing the research paper, and the field is rapidly filling with specialty texts completely devoted to the genre. Many of these texts, particularly the more traditional ones, concentrate heavily on skills such as using the library, taking notes, and documenting sources, together with some standard instructions on outlining and drafting. There is much of value in such discussions. The skills of finding and analyzing sources, of taking useful notes and incorporating them smoothly into a text, of documenting with the needs of the reader in mind, are neither trivial nor mechanical. Yet the mastery of these skills is only a necessary, not a sufficient, condition for becoming a good writer of research papers. Novice research writers also need a sense of how to perform the intricate rhetorical dance illustrated by the dialogue on Kinneavy; a sense of how to incorporate reading into a process that is both rhetorical and epistemic. But instruction on the research process is typically silent on this issue; it deals with the beginning and the end of the process (using the library and writing the drafts), but it has a gaping hole in the middle where much of the real work of knowledge construction is performed. The evaluation of sources is treated chiefly as a matter of measuring the writer's overall authority as a witness to facts, as measured by factors such as his reputation and the recency of the source.

This view places the use of print sources outside the rhetorical act. In many important ways it reflects Socrates's complaint in Plato's *Phaedrus*:

> Writing, you know, Phaedrus, has this strange quality about it, which makes it really like painting: the painter's products stand before us quite as though they were alive; but if you question them, they maintain a solemn silence. So, too, with written words: you might think they spoke as though they made sense, but if you ask them anything about what they are saying, if you wish an explanation, they go on telling you the same thing, over and over forever.[4]

According to this view, print is merely a repository of fossilized rhetorical acts that can no longer actively participate in the living process of rhetoric. Thus research involving secondary sources is seen as only preliminary to, not part of, the process of creating new meaning. The rhetorical model of reading implies that this view is too limited. The goal of instruction must be to help students get research back inside the rhetorical act, a place where more experienced readers (whether or not they consciously know it) routinely place it. Students must learn to see the texts that intervene between them and the subject of their research as more than repositories of data that "maintain a solemn silence" when questioned. They must learn, as Bazerman puts it, to "consider each piece of writing as a contribution to an ongoing, written conversation."[5] They must learn to see them as repositories of alternative ways of knowing, repositories which must be actively interrogated and whose meaning must be constructed, not simply extracted. They must learn to use reading not only to participate vicariously in others' experience, but also to participate in others' interpretations of experience. Most important, they must learn how to select portions of those interpretations to incorporate into their own worldviews and ultimately to pass on to others through writing. In short, they must learn how to be persuaded by texts.

How to Teach It

Teaching students how to be persuaded by texts is obviously not an easy task. Mature researchers clearly learn how to do it somehow; we have seen Crusius, Knoblauch, Hunter, and others sharing knowledge back and forth in a rhetorically sophisticated manner. But can we as teachers intervene to help students acquire this skill with maximum efficiency?

At first glance, the rhetorical model of reading seems to suggest that the ability to read in a rhetorical mode results from processes not amenable to instruction, or at least, not to instruction in a reading and writing class. If a prerequisite for rhetorical reading is a richly stocked repertoire of schemata, it would seem to follow that students cannot be good researchers until they have acquired a satisfactory stock of world knowledge with which to interpret new data. Therefore, students should not undertake research until late in their university careers when they have mastered the basic elements of their discipline. Stephen North makes exactly this argument, claiming that students often have "no depth of knowledge, no existing schema for the subject area in which they are writing."[6] As a result, North concludes that the writing of the research paper should generally be taught only in higher-level courses. Another version of this line of reasoning is that of David Wells, who would teach research in introductory courses but would limit assignments to pure retrieval of information because students at this level do not have the experience to do more. "I regard it as outrageous," Wells comments, "to demand that a typical freshman originate a feasible thesis."[7]

These responses would perhaps be justified if a reader's repertoire consisted solely or even principally of disciplinary knowledge. To be sure, disciplinary knowledge is an indispensable part of disciplinary reading. But the repertoire consists of much more than this. It is a complex system of linguistic information, general as well as disciplinary knowledge, and emotional associations and values. It is not necessary to have a full stock of specific disciplinary knowledge in order to have a repertoire that one can use to interpret and evaluate new knowledge. Most important, the structure of knowledge, associations, and values that makes up a person's repertoire is formed largely by the experience of meeting other worldviews through exchange of discourse. As we have seen, this interchange is goal driven. The way we are persuaded by what we read depends on the questions we ask of the texts we interrogate. As Burke, Booth, and other rhetoricians remind us, we receive information in symbolic interchange with other selves, not just by passively receiving and storing up what others have to offer, but by interacting symbolically with them, participating in Burke's "co-operative competition of the parliamentary." It is, of course, possible to read for simple information retrieval, building up a repertoire of disciplinary knowledge for no immediate purpose other than to pass a test. However, the rhetorical model of reading suggests that this method of stocking a repertoire is severely impoverished. We build and modify our repertoires more actively by participating in the "textual economy" of producing and consuming texts in pursuit of answers to questions—in the academic context, by writing papers based on research. Therefore, to delay immersing students in research until their repertoire is formed is to deny them access to one of the most important of the processes that form it. This is clearly a self-defeating proposition.

The rhetorical model of reading, then, does not tell us to delay teaching research-based writing until students' repertoires are in place. Rather, it tells us that we must help students learn to use their current structures of knowledge as bridges to newer and richer structures of more specifically disciplinary knowledge. In order to do so, they must be able to understand what it means to engage in the social construction rather than the individualistic de-archiving of meaning.

The rhetorical model itself, however, does not tell us exactly how we should do this. How each individual teacher proceeds from a model of mature performance to a procedure for teaching that performance depends to a large extent on that teacher's pedagogical philosophy. Such philosophies typically range on a continuum from the most direct kinds of instruction, such as the venerable reading-lecture-assignment structure, to indirect methods in which students are set tasks that will allow them to discover new knowledge for themselves. Some composition theorists such as Linda Flower believe that even tacit knowledge is often learned cognitively in the initial stages and then gradually internalized. Admitting that "blissful ignorance is, of course, highly functional at times," she also insists that "the trick is being able to rise to both philosophical and metacognitive awareness when one needs to."[8] Others such as Knoblauch and Brannon and Russell Hunt insist that direct instruction is at best useless and possibly harmful, since it makes students consciously aware of activities that can only proceed efficiently when unconscious.[9]

Although I have my own ideas on the subject (which will not be hard to infer from what follows), my purpose here is not to enter directly into the debate over which point on this continuum offers the best possibilities of producing useful pedagogy. Rather, I wish to offer a set of examples, suggestive rather than exhaustive in nature, of how both direct and indirect methods of pedagogy could be used to impart the skill of rhetorical reading in the context of research-based writing. These methods fall into two broad groups: *telling* about the process of research and *constructing activities* to help students internalize research skills. These categories do not precisely correspond to the distinction between direct and indirect instruction—teachers can construct activities to get students to practice what they have been told directly—but it provides a useful way of grouping two distinct types of pedagogical activity.

1. Telling

Simply telling students how to perform any task, from throwing a basketball to writing a research paper, obviously will not by itself enable them to perform it. Telling is a highly efficient means of imparting *knowledge*, but it is highly suspect as a means of imparting a *skill*. This does not mean, however, that it has no value as part of a pedagogical program. Flower suggests how this may occur:

> From an educational point of view, the small entity labelled "awareness" is more than a luxury option. We can, of course, influence the process of reading and writing indirectly through assignments, feedback, and grades. But we can often expand a thinking process most quickly by giving students a window on their own cognitive acts—especially when those acts appear to be highly determined by one force or another. We can help students become aware of their own strategies and we can teach other strategies we value, provided, of course, that we ourselves understand the process we would teach.[10]

If Flower and other proponents of direct teaching methods are right that it is helpful to open a "window" on a cognitive act—and I think that they are at least partly right—then we can improve the way students do research simply by telling them more about what it means to do it. Too often, we treat the purpose of research as self-evident. We tell students the nuts and bolts of research—how to take notes, how to write a footnote—but we forget to tell them why they are doing it. It is so obvious to us that, as Michael Polanyi would say, it has passed from focal to tacit knowledge,[11] and we are no longer aware of the complex reasons why we select certain materials to include in a research paper and reject others; why we choose to quote here, paraphrase there, and, in still other cases, get the ideas from our reading so entangled with our own that extricating them is not only impossible but meaningless. We can perhaps save students from some of the worst pitfalls simply by explaining some of the points about reading and writing that I have elaborated in this book. Of these, I would rate the following as particularly important:

a. *The purpose of research is not simply to retrieve data but to participate in a conversation about it.* Understanding this goal (so easy to state, so difficult to achieve) may help students set the sort of high-level goals that we unconsciously set for our own research. We must, of course, understand that this *is* a very high-level goal, and that beginners will not reach more than a pale approximation of it. But students who reproduce perfect summaries of their sources are often bewildered by the damningly faint praise they receive. The rhetorical model of reading can provide the vocabulary we need to explain more clearly why summaries are not research, and what students should be aiming for.

b. *There is no such thing as an unbiased source.* The word "bias" has become a term of condemnation: to call a source "biased" is usually taken as sufficient grounds to reject it out of hand. Yet, as we have seen, writers make the claims they do for very complex and individual reasons—reasons that readers can learn to unpack and evaluate. At the very least, understanding why sources can differ so radically on even seemingly objective matters can help ease some of the bewilderment (often shading into outrage) that students feel when they notice these disagreements.

c. *Feelings can be a source of shareable good reasons for belief.* Students often throw up their hands in despair when confronted by sources making opposing claims, and report either an irreconcilable conflict or an empty conclusion such as "I believe that X is right, not Y," without supporting evidence. Yet, when pressed, they often find that they do have feelings that a certain source is somehow more worthy of belief than another, and, when pressed further, they can often explain why. The explanation often turns out to be the sorts of criteria that I have labeled "ethos" or "pathos," criteria which students have been trained to distrust. But, as the dialogue on Kinneavy illustrates, these sorts of gut reactions can be teased out, explored, and turned into evidence that can be put down on paper as valid means of persuading a reader to share one's beliefs. Students must come to understand Booth's doctrine that "every desire, every feeling, can become a good reason when called into the court of symbolic exchange."[12]

d. *Research is recursive.* Too many students assume, and too many teachers and textbooks imply, that a good researcher should be able to glean everything she needs from a book, make careful notes, and then put the book back on the shelf and never look at it again. We must tell students what our own experience tells us: that the questions they are asking of a source will mature and shift as they read, and will develop further when they begin writing and rewriting their papers. Questions they never thought to ask the first time will drive them back into their material and into new material as often and as deeply as their energy and schedules permit. A writer who begins with a question such as "What were the causes of the War of 1812?" may find that as her research proceeds she becomes involved with a slightly different question, such as "What was the relationship between the revolutionary nations such as the U.S. and France and the non-revolutionary nations such as England?" The new question will send the reader back to new sources, and back to the same sources with a different set of eyes that will evoke a new virtual work from them. This is more than the typical "narrowing" of a subject to make it more "manageable," a step usually treated as preliminary. It is a recognition that evoking meaning from texts is a recursive, not a linear process.

These suggestions do not, of course, exhaust the pedagogical lessons of the rhetorical model of reading. But they outline some of the more important aspects of the process that I believe students need to be told. They not only provide substance for lectures (a notoriously impoverished method of teaching discourse skills), but also provide the background for more meaningful feedback, both oral and written, to students as they work through drafts and after they have turned in finished assignments. Generating such feedback makes up a good deal of any teacher's workload, and many feel that students learn more from it than from any other single instructional tool. Yet without a clear idea of what we want students to achieve, and even more important, without a clear idea of what strategies might help them achieve it, comments tend to degenerate into marginal grunting (Awk! Dev! Coh!) that conveys displeasure with a finished product without suggesting how to improve the process that led to it. The rhetorical model of reading suggests specific advice that we can give students when their product suggests that their process is falling short.

Let me illustrate with a specific example. A student named Anne came to me for one-to-one tutoring in my institution's writing center, referred by a professor in a history course. She brought with her a paper on the early fur trade in Canada, on which she had received a "C." Aside from some stylistic infelicities, the main problem that the history professor had noted was that she had not supported her claims with evidence. For instance, she claimed that the fur traders had not done much to protect the native peoples and had not made any effort to improve their standard of living; they had merely taken their furs and left them to their own devices. However, she did not say why she believed this.

When I asked her why she believed it, Anne replied that nine of the ten sources she had consulted presented versions of the claim. But interestingly, she believed the nine sources over the one, not just because of numerical superiority, but also because, as she put it, "What I know about the treatment of native people in general leads me to suppose it wasn't much different then." She had evaluated the specialized knowledge of her sources, not by connecting it with other specialized knowledge—she was too new to the field of Canadian History to possess much—but rather by connecting it to much more generalized knowledge. The claim under investigation had fit with a generalized schema for the way natives are treated—a schema abstracted from everything from the daily newspaper to a half-remembered reading of *Bury My Heart at Wounded Knee*. In more rhetorical terms, it had achieved an enthymemic connection with doxai that were already in place. But because she didn't know consciously what she had done, she was unable to turn the process around and use it explicitly as a source of proof when she turned from a being a reader to being a writer. The claim simply sat as an unsupported generalization. This is a dramatic illustration of Wayne Booth's assertion that one good reason for belief is "coherence with other kinds of knowledge."[13] But there is more to the story. Upon questioning, Anne revealed that the general question of how the natives were treated turned on a more specific issue. Under the terms of its mandate from the government, the Hudson's Bay Company was obligated to establish missions along the Fraser River for the benefit of the native peoples. (Just how much actual benefit such missions would have been is, of course, quite another question.) One report said that such missions existed and another said they did not. Both of these reports were historical documents—"primary" sources claiming to be eyewitness accounts, not later interpretations. Flummoxed by such basic contradictions of fact, Anne had simply avoided going deeply into the issue at all. The debate appeared in her paper simply as an unresolved conflict. "What am I to do," she asked helplessly, "when sources completely contradict each other like that?"

Yet the criteria for judgment were, in this case, not hard to find. The source that claimed the missions existed was the Hudson's Bay Company itself; the source that contradicted the claim was a federal government report critical of the activities of the fur industry. Once asked which of these sources would be the more reliable on such a question, Anne saw that the company would be more likely to be self-serving. This was a relatively clear-cut case that did not require fine distinctions about what "unbiased" really means, what are the limits of observation, how people can have alternate modes of meaning, and so on. It was a paradigm case of lying and truth. Yet she simply was not operating in a mode that allowed her to bring these considerations of ethos to bear on the situation. She could not see that the same criteria that would tell her whether or not to believe that her little brother had swiped a cookie could be brought to bear on a question of history.

The history professor had noted the lack of evidence for claims, but had interpreted it as a lack of sheer *volume* of reading (as it might have been if a trained reader in history had been caught in the same sin). His global comment was, "Seems a bit thin. Perhaps a more extensive bibliography would have helped." In fact, she had over twenty titles in her bibliography, more than enough for a junior-level paper. She just had not been able to construct defensible claims from them.

Admittedly, the sort of probing I have described works far better in individual conferences than in marginal commentary. Instruction by telling is effective in direct ratio to the individuality of the telling, on an ascending scale from lecture to group discussion to marginal commentary to individual conferences. However, an awareness of how interpretations are built and evaluated might have helped Anne's professor generate comments that questioned much more closely the reasons for Anne's claims and offered some suggestions as to how to find ways of supporting them. Certainly it might have spared Anne the unhelpful advice to go away and do even more reading when she had not been able to make good use of what she had already done.

2. *Constructing Activities*

Telling, of course, can only be a preparation for doing. An understanding of the rhetorical forces at work in research should guide not only what is said in the various modes of direct instruction, but also the way teachers construct assignments and classroom activities in order to encourage a rhetorical view of research.

First, since good research is recursive, necessitating many passes through the same material (and often many physical trips to the library), teachers must allow sufficient time for students to refine their questions and give them step-by-step encouragement to do so. In their paper "The Road Not Taken: How the Writing Context Influences Students' Choices," Jennie Nelson and John R. Hayes contrast two types of research strategy typically employed by students.[14] One type, which Nelson and Hayes call "low-investment strategies," involves techniques such as racing quickly through the first dozen books available to glean raw information in a single pass. "High-investment strategies," in contrast, involve techniques such as rereading sources in the light of refined questions. Nelson and Hayes claim that the students who choose high-investment strategies are typically those who are encouraged to do so by specific pedagogical techniques. A teacher who sets a research assignment well in advance, encourages students to record the progress of their ideas as they develop, and meets with them individually before they hand in their final drafts will have the opportunity to sound out their research strategies and motivate them to go back to their sources if the direction of their inquiry seems to be changing.

Anne had used a low-investment strategy without even realizing that high-investment strategies existed. Having made a few blanket statements about her subject and found them difficult to support, she should have been willing to go back to her sources—possibly new sources, possibly the same ones evoked differently under the direction of a new question—and find the support. In fact, the first assignment I gave her in the writing center was to take one of her unsupported generalizations, return to the library, and come back with it turned into a supportable claim. But as Nelson and Hayes point out, and Anne's experience confirms, students will not use these higher-investment strategies (even if they are aware of them) unless the timing and structure of the assignment encourages them to do so.

My experience with Anne is an example of highly individualized instruction. However, my entire claim in this book is that knowledge is socially constructed. This suggests that at least some, if not all, elements of classroom practice should be social rather than individualistic or one-to-one. The interactions between student and sources, and student and teacher can be supplemented by a third interaction: between student and student.

Collaborative learning is a popular pedagogical tool that grows directly out of a social view of knowledge. In *Invention as a Social Act*, for instance, Karen Burke LeFevre argues for an expanded view of rhetorical invention that is in many ways similar to mine.[15] Because she sees invention in this larger context, as a participation in a rhetorical interchange among texts rather than as an "atomistic" process of individual contemplation, LeFevre concludes that composition pedagogy should include group authorship. Students, LeFevre claims, should be given opportunities to form research communities within the classroom. By collaborating on research projects, reading and evaluating texts, and constructing new texts together, students will learn to form the types of social relationships in which knowledge is typically constructed outside of the classroom.

Kenneth Bruffee's work on collaborative learning also recognizes the relationship between reading/writing and the epistemic conversation. In "Collaborative Learning and the 'Conversation of Mankind,'" Bruffee develops an analogy between writing and conversation:

> Writing is a technologically displaced form of conversation. When
> we write, having already internalized the "skill and partnership" of
> conversation, we displace it once more onto the written page.[16]

This conversational view of invention leads Bruffee, like LeFevre, to
recommend teaching students to write in a collaborative mode:

> The inference writing teachers should take from this line of reasoning
> is that our task must involve engaging students in conversation
> among themselves at as many points in both the writing and the
> reading process as possible, and that we should contrive to ensure
> that students' conversation about what they read and write is similar
> in as many ways as possible to the way we would like them eventu-
> ally to read and write.[17]

At St. Thomas University in New Brunswick, Canada, teacher/
researchers such as James A. Reither, Douglas Vipond, and Russell A.
Hunt have developed some innovative ways of putting these ideas into
practice by turning an entire classroom into an active research community.[18] Reither states that the goal of such courses is to "immerse students
in academic knowledge/discourse communities so that they can write
from within those communities."[19] The course is designed to involve the
entire class in a single research project and to get the students working
together to solve it using all the methods of research available, including
both primary and secondary sources:

> Organizing a course in this way allows an incredible range of reading
> activities—in everything from bibliographies to books; and a similar
> range of writing activities—from jotting down call numbers to
> writing formal articles of the sorts they are reading. . . . The inquiry
> is made manageable in the same way all such inquiries are made
> manageable, not by "choosing" and "focussing" a topic, but by
> seeking answers to the questions which impel the investigation.[20]

Reither, in short, recommends embedding all the reading and writing
activities we want our students to learn in a single overarching context,
rather than teaching them in bits and pieces in separate decontextualized
activities. This method is particularly appealing because of its emphasis
on creating a rhetorical context containing real goals that are free to shift
during the course of the project. Thus it engages one of the most
important aspects of the rhetorical model of reading. Moreover, because
the discourse community model requires that students pursue the same
project for a long period of time, possibly an entire term, it provides the
time for students to find their way toward the "high-investment"
strategies recommended by Nelson and Hayes.

If we believe proponents of the "discourse community" method such as Reither, Vipond, and Hunt, students in such classes will automatically learn to read and write rhetorically because they will be engaged in a context in which these activities are constantly going on:

> Except on an ad hoc basis, at "teaching points," the instructor does not attempt to teach research or writing skills explicitly. The students learn most of what they need to know about inquiry, reading and writing as part of the larger process of joining a post-secondary, academic version of what Frank Smith calls the "literary club."[21]

The students will internalize rhetorical reading in the same way as Crusius, Knoblauch, and Hunter have presumably internalized it: by doing it.

Other teachers, however, may want to design more directive and less global activities that focus more specifically on the subskills that make up the overarching skill of rhetorical reading. Bazerman, for instance, suggests that students be asked to compare the claims and evidence of a number of different sources and evaluate the kind and degree of agreement and disagreement.[22] This activity could be extended into a collaborative mode by dividing students into groups and giving each group a text to read and discuss. The rhetorical model of reading predicts that they will construct different and sometimes contradictory virtual works. There must be an element of coherence and predictability in a rhetorical transaction or the transaction ceases to be rhetorical at all; it is therefore reasonable to compare readings and eliminate some as being clearly too far from what one would normally expect to be the author's intention.

However, this process could be taken too far. An extreme version of this pedagogy would require students to synthesize these readings into a single definitive reading, paring down differences between readings until a consensual virtual work can be constructed. The rhetorical model of reading suggests that this approach overstates the degree of consensus that normally occurs as reality is socially constructed. Rhetorical negotiation does not mean eliminating differences until a sort of interpretive entropy is reached at the point of consensus. Rather, it means using the differences between people in an exploratory fashion to improve and update our knowledge. Consequently, groups of students could be set to the task, not of eliminating disagreements, but of exploring what in their own experience of the world and their own values has led them to construct their varied interpretations. By detailed comparison of each other's readings, students can begin to get in touch with the processes by which they understand texts, and begin to grasp the relationship between different repertoires and different virtual works. At the same time, they can explore the factors that set limits on interpretation: the commonalities of human experience and of factual knowledge that the writer can use to predict response.

I have claimed that as well as constructing an abstract and ever-shifting virtual work, readers must also use a complex and highly personal set of criteria in order to judge that work and set it in a useful relation to other works. I have framed my model of these criteria in terms of the three classical pisteis. Group activities should help students learn how to balance all three of these standards of judgment and use them as evidence to persuade readers.

To apprehend fully the process of logos, students must work toward discovering how their own doxai allow them to evaluate a work at the same time as the work is persuading them to modify their own doxai. One student may reach a positive judgment of a particular writer's conclusions because the lines of argument the writer uses tie into the student's prior understanding of the world. Another may reject the work because its acceptance would require the alteration of too many deeply held beliefs without a corresponding gain in the coherence of his understanding of the world. By comparing each other's judgments, students can work toward understanding how their own doxai affect their own judgments, as Anne, in the example above, did with her belief about the treatment of native peoples by the early fur traders. Once they understand how this process works, they will be better equipped to answer the more difficult question of whether they should reject the work or modify their doxai. Only by understanding which of their own beliefs are the most deeply held, as well as the reasons for this relative tenacity of belief, can students progress from an instinctive favoring of one text over another to a conscious, rational process of deciding when to change their minds.

Students must also understand how they can use their emotional as well as their rational reactions to sources. Too often students are told to separate "fact" from "opinion," advice which explicitly or implicitly encourages them to value the former and discount the latter. To some extent this advice is useful. Students must learn to avoid being overwhelmed by powerful and immediate emotional judgments—they must not, for instance, automatically reject an assertion as untrue because they do not approve of its consequences. However, they must also learn not to attempt to expel emotional reactions from the process of judgment. That is, they must avoid what Booth calls the "fact-value split" by learning to use their emotional apprehension of value as one part of a complex judgmental process. This too can be set as one of the goals of group evaluation of texts.

The rhetorical model of reading suggests that ethos, the systematic complex of beliefs and values that I have called the writer's "textual character," is also a highly important factor in persuasion. Accordingly, while they are probing each other's reactions to sources, students should also be encouraged to construct and use the ethos of the writers of sources. Teachers can encourage students to ask the same questions that the participants in the dialogue on Kinneavy ask of Kinneavy and of each other. That is, they can encourage their students to attempt to characterize the philosophical mindset, the textual personality, that lies behind the conclusions that authors draw from their information. Here it may be helpful to supply sets of material by the same authors. By attempting to trace consistencies in outlook among several texts by the same author, as I did with three of Knoblauch's texts in chapter 4, students can begin to understand how beliefs can be coherent structures through which readers see the world, not just isolated "biases" that can be stripped away from the "facts."

This sort of exercise can turn into a form of dialogic criticism as discussed in the previous chapter. There, I offered an extended example of dialogic criticism partly to show the rhetorical model of reading in action and partly to show how such criticism could, in Black's words, improve our understanding of the human mind "through the investigation and appraisal of the activities and products of men."[23] Imported into the classroom, this sort of criticism can become a form of modeling. By analyzing a series of authors wrestling with the same problem, constructing different views of a phenomenon, questioning and answering each other, and offering different sorts of evidence for their beliefs, students can achieve a clearer picture of what they might be able to do themselves. Such criticism, of course, can only be treated as groundwork; watching others' processes secondhand can never substitute for trying them out oneself. But at the very least, this form of analysis can validate the emotional and ethical forms of proof that students have been conditioned to deny, and so open an avenue for learning to use those forms.

Collaborative learning, then, can help students learn how reading fits into the larger processes of rhetorical invention and how they can use specific strategies to interrogate and evaluate their sources. It is up to the individual teacher to decide whether to guide the activity of these groups closely or to let students discover for themselves how rhetorical communities operate. As I have said, the rhetorical model of reading as invention does not in itself predict how we teach it. But it can, as we have seen, suggest a pedagogical direction by virtue of its account of mature performance—its model of what expert readers do when confronted by multiple texts offering multiple interpretations of the world. It is this model that can turn the knack of teaching research into an art of helping students learn to read, not just as retrievers of data, but as complex human beings in Weaver's sense: not just as logic machines, but as human beings who both judge and advise with their whole logical, aesthetic, and ethical beings.

Implications for the Art of Rhetoric

In the introduction, I claimed that another reason for developing a rhetoric of reading was to expand the art of rhetoric in order to account more fully for new views of the role of persuasion in the creation of knowledge. Having developed such a rhetoric of reading and examined its implications for rhetorical criticism and for teaching, I would like to return to the more general implications of this model from a broadened and more detailed perspective. I want to ask not just why rhetoric *needs to* include a rhetoric of reading—the question that guided chapter 1—but also what the inclusion of a rhetoric of reading *does for* rhetoric. In other words, what do we now know about the rhetorical process that we did not know before developing a model of how reading can be understood as one of its subprocesses?

First, an expanded definition of persuasion leads to an expanded definition of invention. Persuasion has always been central to the art of rhetoric. However, modern rhetoricians such as Wayne Booth and Kenneth Burke emphasize the role of persuasion not only in the passing on of knowledge from one person to another, but also in the development and perfection of knowledge, and in the creation of the self through intercourse with other selves. Burke's classic metaphor of the unending conversation illustrates the way in which we create and attempt to perfect knowledge by attempting to persuade others of the validity of propositions. As Wayne Booth points out, this view of knowledge as created in rhetoric means that "the supreme purpose of persuasion . . . could not be to talk someone else into a preconceived view; rather it must be to engage in mutual inquiry or exploration."[24]

The office of invention, then, has been expanded to include not only the finding of arguments to support a position, but the finding of the position itself—a position that must be perceived as provisional, for attaining it is merely a starting point in a process that will surely modify it as the conversation proceeds. Therefore invention must be seen as a Janus-headed process. It looks backward to previous stages of the conversation that offer the rhetor others' provisional forms of knowledge; at the same time, it looks forward to the audience to which the rhetor will present her knowledge, her best estimate of the world at the time of composing the piece of discourse in question.

Having developed an account of rhetorical invention that takes account of this expanded view of the process, we not only know *that*, as Booth argues, we are creatures "made in rhetoric"; we know *how*. A rhetoric of reading thus helps fulfill Wayne Booth's search for "grounds for confidence in a multiplicity of ways of knowing."[25] The close relationship between a person's particular configuration of doxai and the degree to which she will be persuaded by any given piece of discourse explains the wide diversity in human belief. It provides a set of principles that can answer the puzzling question of how different intelligent people can read the same sources and reach apparently contradictory conclusions. By grounding the process of reaching a conclusion in a highly variable process of constructing a virtual work, the model also accounts for the way different readers not only reach different conclusions about source texts but also appear to have read different texts.

Confidence in a multiplicity of ways of knowing requires an understanding not only of how we construct, but also of how we come to believe or reject the propositions presented by this virtual work. The rhetorical model of reading provides this account through its reevaluation of the enthymeme, the most fundamental working principle of traditional rhetoric. From the point of view of a rhetoric of reading rather than a rhetoric of composition, the principle of the enthymeme operates on what might be called an input rather than an output level. In composing discourse, the enthymeme is a method by which the rhetor as composer, by emphasizing the connections between his and his audience's doxai, shapes the discourse in ways that will make it maximally acceptable to the audience. However, in reading discourse, the enthymeme becomes a means by which the rhetor as reader selects the propositions that he will add to his own store of knowledge. The propositions which are accepted are those which make the most coherent logical, emotional, and ethical connections with the reader's repertoire of knowledge. In short, because it describes the mechanism by which knowledge is both received and transmitted, the enthymeme may be seen as the pivot upon which turns the entire process of creating knowledge through rhetorical interchange.

However, the rhetorical model of reading also reminds us that, despite the attractiveness of electronic metaphors such as receiving and transmitting, the enthymeme is not a mechanical process. It is simply an abstract concept that helps account for a humane process. The doxai that the enthymeme works with are the opinions of human beings—provisional, changeable, and, as the division of proof into the pisteis reminds us, influenced not just by logic but by emotion and character. By suggesting in detail how doxai form bridges of identification between human beings, the model establishes a holistic view of knowledge that fulfills and extends the view of the human being asserted by modern rhetoricians such as Weaver.

In addition, a rhetorical view of reading provides insights into the balance between shared and unshareable components of discourse. It is essential to understand the role of individual personality, biography, and rhetorical situation in the construction of belief systems, for it is these factors that enable us to account for the diversity of human belief. But as we have seen, it is also important to understand the sources of constraint on belief that grow out of shared communal and universal values. These constraints—the conventional meanings of words, the similarities among interpretive communities that grow out of the commonalities of human experience, the assumption that systems of belief strive for maximum internal consistency—provide the basis for educated predictions as to how another will react to a given piece of discourse. Conversely, they provide the basis for educated guesses as to the genesis and structure of others' belief systems.

Thus, a rhetoric of reading provides grounds for confidence not only in a multiplicity of ways of knowing, but also in our ability to understand each others' ways of knowing. If we can understand the ways people can be led to opposite conclusions by what appear to be the same facts, we have a basis for putting into practice the principles of mutual inquiry and exploration under which, in Wayne Booth's rhetoric, persuasion is subsumed.

It is one of the fundamental, if often unspoken, assumptions of academic inquiry that to understand a process is to achieve some form of control over it. If rhetoric can help us understand not just the way knowledge is transmitted but also, through an expanded account of invention, the way it is made through verbal interaction, it can help us understand how we build ourselves and our understanding of the world. If we can understand this, perhaps we can also understand how to sort through the seemingly infinite variety of jostling opinions that clamor for our assent and to identify in a principled way the ones that are worthy of having influence on our belief systems—to control, that is, in a nonarbitrary way, the formation of our beliefs.

In the conclusion of their treatise on practical argumentation, Perelman and Olbrechts-Tyteca suggest how far the implications of such understanding can reach:

> If freedom was no more than necessary adherence to a previously
> given natural order, it would exclude all possibility of choice; and if
> the exercise of freedom were not based on reasons, every choice
> would be irrational and would be reduced to an arbitrary decision

operating in an intellectual void. It is because of the possibility of argumentation which provides reasons, but not compelling reasons, that it is possible to escape the dilemma: adherence to an objectively and universally valid truth, or recourse to suggestion and violence to secure acceptance for our opinions and decisions.[26]

What Perelman and Olbrechts-Tyteca claim for argumentation—the production of arguments based on reasons—may also be claimed for its logical counterpart, a rhetorical account of the uptake of arguments. Only if we can understand how to base our beliefs on a logical, emotional, and ethical response—not just to propositions in the abstract but to others' belief systems—can we hope to avoid the dilemma to which Perelman and Olbrechts-Tyteca draw our attention. The understanding provided by a rhetoric of reading can help us build belief systems based neither on absolute truth nor on arbitrary selection from equally valid propositions, but on good reasons and informed free choice.

Notes

1. Richard Larson, "The 'Research Paper' in the Writing Course: A Non-Form of Writing," *College English, 44* (1982): 813.

2. James E. Ford and Dennis R. Perry, "Research Paper Instruction in the Undergraduate Writing Program," *College English, 44* (1982): 827.

3. James E. Ford, et al., "Selected Bibliography on Research Paper Instruction," *Literary Research Newsletter, 6* (1981): 51.

4. Plato, *Phaedrus,* trans. W. C. Helmbold and W. G. Rabinowitz (Indianapolis: Bobbs-Merrill, 1956), 69.

5. Charles Bazerman, "A Relationship between Reading and Writing: The Conversational Model," *College English, 41* (1980): 657.

6. Stephen North, "Teaching Research Writing: Five Criteria," *Freshman English News, 9* (1980): 18.

7. David M. Wells, "A Program for the Freshman Research Paper," *College Composition and Communication, 28* (1977): 383.

8. Linda Flower, "Interpretive Acts: Cognition and the Construction of Discourse," *Poetics, 16* (1987): 112.

9. See C. H. Knoblauch and Lil Brannon, *Rhetorical Traditions and the Teaching of Writing* (Upper Montclair: Boynton/Cook, 1984), and Russell A. Hunt, "A Horse Named Hans, A Boy Named Shawn: The Herr von Osten Theory of Response to Writing," in *Writing and Response: Theory, Practice, and Research,* ed. Chris M. Anson (Urbana: National Council of Teachers of English, 1989), 80–100.

10. Flower, 113.

11. See Michael Polanyi, *Personal Knowledge: Towards a Post-Critical Philosophy* (Chicago: University of Chicago Press, 1958).

12. Wayne C. Booth, *Modern Dogma and the Rhetoric of Assent* (Chicago: University of Chicago Press, 1974), 120.

13. Booth, 164.

14. Jennie Nelson and John R. Hayes, "The Road Not Taken: How The Writing Context Influences Students' Choices." Paper read at the Conference on College Composition and Communication, St. Louis, 1988.

15. Karen Burke LeFevre, *Invention as a Social Act* (Carbondale: Southern Illinois University Press, 1987).

16. Kenneth A. Bruffee, "Collaborative Learning and the 'Conversation of Mankind,'" *College English, 46* (1984): 641.

17. Bruffee, 642.

18. See James A. Reither, "Writing and Knowing: Toward Redefining the Writing Process," *College English, 47* (1985): 620–28, and James A. Reither and Douglas Vipond, "Writing as Collaboration," *College English, 51* (1989): 855–67.

19. Reither, 624.

20. Reither, 625-26.

21. Reither and Vipond, 863.

22. Bazerman, 660.

23. Edwin Black, *Rhetorical Criticism: A Study in Method* (Madison: University of Wisconsin Press, 1978), 9.

24. Booth, 137.

25. Booth, 99.

26. Chaim Perelman and L. Olbrechts-Tyteca, *The New Rhetoric: A Treatise on Argumentation*, trans. John Wilkinson and Purcell Weaver (Notre Dame: University of Notre Dame Press, 1969), 514.

Works Cited

Anderson, Richard C. "The Notion of Schemata and the Educational Enterprise: General Discussion of the Conference." In *Schooling and the Acquisition of Knowledge.* Ed. Richard C. Anderson, Rand J. Spiro, and William E. Montague, 415–31. Hillsdale: Erlbaum, 1977.

Anderson, Richard C., et al. "Frameworks for Comprehending Discourse." *American Educational Research Journal, 14* (1977): 367–81.

Aristotle. *Rhetoric.* Trans. Lane Cooper. Englewood Cliffs: Prentice-Hall, 1932.

Augustine, Saint. *On Christian Doctrine.* Trans. D. W. Robertson. Indianapolis: Bobbs-Merrill, 1958.

Bazerman, Charles. "A Relationship between Reading and Writing: The Conversational Model." *College English, 41* (1980): 656–61.

Bitzer, Lloyd. "The Rhetorical Situation." In *Contemporary Theories of Rhetoric: Selected Readings.* Ed. Richard L. Johannesen, 381–93. New York: Harper, 1971.

Black, Edwin. *Rhetorical Criticism: A Study in Method.* Madison: University of Wisconsin Press, 1978.

Bleich, David. *Subjective Criticism.* Baltimore: Johns Hopkins University Press, 1978.

Booth, Wayne C. *Modern Dogma and the Rhetoric of Assent.* Chicago: University of Chicago Press, 1974.

———. *The Rhetoric of Fiction.* 2nd ed. Chicago: University of Chicago Press, 1983.

Brown, Gillian, and George Yule. *Discourse Analysis.* Cambridge: Cambridge University Press, 1983.

Bruffee, Kenneth A. "Collaborative Learning and the 'Conversation of Mankind.'" *College English, 46* (1984): 635–52.

Bryant, Donald C. *Rhetorical Dimensions in Criticism.* Baton Rouge: Louisiana State University Press, 1973.

Burke, Kenneth. *Counter-Statement.* Berkeley: University of California Press, 1931.

———. *Language as Symbolic Action.* Berkeley: University of California Press, 1966.

———. *The Philosophy of Literary Form: Studies in Symbolic Action.* Berkeley: University of California Press, 1941.

———. *A Rhetoric of Motives.* Berkeley: University of California Press, 1950.

Campbell, George. *The Philosophy of Rhetoric.* Ed. Lloyd F. Bitzer. Carbondale: Southern Illinois University Press, 1963.

Carey, Robert F., and Jerome C. Harste. "Comprehension as Context: Toward Reconsideration of a Transactional Theory of Reading." In *Understanding Readers' Understanding: Theory and Practice.* Ed. Robert J. Tierney, Patricia L. Anders, and Judy Nichols Mitchell, 189–204. Hillsdale: Erlbaum, 1987.

Cicero. *De Oratore*. Trans. E. W. Sutton and H. Rackham. 2 vols. Cambridge: Loeb-Harvard University Press, 1976.

Corbett, Edward J. "The *Topoi* Revisited." In *Rhetoric and Praxis: The Contribution of Classical Rhetoric to Practical Reasoning*. Ed. Jean Dietz Moss, 43–58. Washington: Catholic University of America Press, 1986.

Corder, Jim W. "Rhetorical Analysis of Writing." In *Teaching Composition: Ten Bibliographical Essays*. Ed. Gary Tate, 223–40. Fort Worth: Texas Christian University Press, 1976.

Crusius, Timothy W. "A Brief Plea for a Paradigm and for Kinneavy as Paradigm."*Freshman English News*, 12.3 (1983): 1–3.

———. "A Comment on 'that we have divided / In three our Kingdom': The Communication Triangle and *A Theory of Discourse*." *College English*, 49 (1987): 214–19.

———. "Thinking (and Rethinking) Kinneavy." *Rhetoric Review, 3* (1985): 120–30.

Culler, Jonathan. *The Pursuit of Signs: Semiotics, Literature, Deconstruction*. Ithaca: Cornell University Press, 1981.

D'Angelo, Frank J. "Modes of Discourse." In *Teaching Composition: Ten Bibliographical Essays*. Ed. Gary Tate, 111–35. Fort Worth: Texas Christian University Press, 1976.

De Beaugrande, Robert. "Design Criteria for Process Models of Reading." *Reading Research Quarterly, 2* (1981): 261–315.

———. "Text, Attention, and Memory in Reading Research." *Understanding Readers' Understanding: Theory and Practice*. Ed. Robert J. Tierney, Patricia L. Anders, and Judy Nichols Mitchell, 15–58. Hillsdale: Erlbaum, 1987.

Flower, Linda. "Interpretive Acts: Cognition and the Construction of Discourse." *Poetics, 16* (1987): 106–130.

———. "The Construction of Purpose in Writing and Reading." *College English*, 50 (1988): 528–50.

Fish, Stanley. *Is There a Text In This Class? The Authority of Interpretive Communities*. Cambridge: Harvard University Press, 1980.

Ford, James E., et al. "Selected Bibliography on Research Paper Instruction." *Literary Research Newsletter, 6* (1981): 49–65.

Ford, James E., and Dennis R. Perry. "Research Paper Instruction in the Undergraduate Writing Program." *College English, 44* (1982): 825–31.

Gage, John T. "An Adequate Epistemology for Composition: Classical and Modern Perspectives." In *Essays on Classical Rhetoric and Modern Discourse*. Ed. Robert J. Connors, Lisa S. Ede, and Andrea A. Lunsford, 152–69. Carbondale: Southern Illinois University Press, 1984.

Gilbert, Nigel G., and Michael Mulkay. *Opening Pandora's Box: A Sociological Analysis of Scientists' Discourse*. Cambridge: Cambridge University Press, 1984.

Goetz, Ernest T., and Bonnie B. Armbruster. "Psychological Correlates of Text Structure." In *Theoretical Issues in Reading Comprehension: Perspectives from Cognitive Psychology, Linguistics, Artificial Intelligence, and Education*. Ed. Rand J. Spiro, Bertram C. Bruce, and William F. Brewer. 201–20. Hillsdale: Erlbaum, 1980.

Grimaldi, William M. A., S. J. *Studies in the Philosophy of Aristotle's Rhetoric.* Weisbaden: Hermes, 1972.

Harrington, Elbert W. *Rhetoric and the Scientific Method of Inquiry: A Study of Invention.* Boulder: University of Colorado Press, 1948.

Hunt, Russell A. "A Horse Named Hans, A Boy Named Shawn: The Herr von Osten Theory of Response to Writing." In *Writing and Response: Theory, Practice, and Research.* Ed. Chris M. Anson, 80–100. Urbana: National Council of Teachers of English, 1989.

Hunter, Paul. "Paul Hunter Responds [to Timothy W. Crusius]." *College English,* 49 (1987): 219–21.

——. "'that we have divided / In three our Kingdom': The Communication Triangle and *A Theory of Discourse.*" *College English,* 48 (1986): 279–87.

Iser, Wolfgang. *The Act of Reading: A Theory of Aesthetic Response.* Baltimore: Johns Hopkins University Press, 1978.

——. "Reader-Response and the *Pathos* Principle." *Rhetoric Review, 6* (1988): 152–66.

Johnson, Thomas S. "A Comment on 'Collaborative Learning and the "Conversation of Mankind."'" *College English,* 48 (1986): 76.

Kantz, Margaret. "Toward A Pedagogically Useful Theory of Literary Reading." *Poetics, 16* (1987): 155–68.

Kennedy, George A. *Classical Rhetoric and Its Christian and Secular Tradition from Ancient to Modern Times.* Chapel Hill: University of North Carolina Press, 1980.

Kinneavy, James. *A Theory of Discourse: The Aims of Discourse.* New York: Norton, 1971.

Knoblauch, C. H. "Intentionality in the Writing Process: A Case Study." *College Composition and Communication, 31* (1980): 153–59.

——. "Modern Composition Theory and the Rhetorical Tradition." *Freshman English News, 9.2* (1980): 3–17.

Knoblauch, C. H., and Lil Brannon. *Rhetorical Traditions and the Teaching of Writing.* Upper Montclair: Boynton/Cook, 1984.

Kuhn, Thomas S. *The Structure of Scientific Revolutions.* 2nd ed. Chicago: University of Chicago Press, 1970.

Larson, Richard L. "The 'Research Paper' in the Writing Course: A Non-Form of Writing." *College English,* 44 (1982): 811–16.

LeFevre, Karen Burke. *Invention as a Social Act.* Carbondale: Southern Illinois University Press, 1987.

McCormick, Kathleen, and Gary E. Waller. "Text, Reader, Ideology: The Interactive Nature of the Reading Situation." *Poetics, 16* (1987): 193–208.

Mead, George Herbert. *Mind, Self and Society from the Standpoint of a Social Behaviorist.* Ed. Charles W. Morris. Chicago: University of Chicago Press, 1934.

Mervis, Carolyn B. "Category Structure and the Development of Categorization." In *Theoretical Issues in Reading Comprehension: Perspectives from Cognitive Psychology, Linguistics, Artificial Intelligence, and Education.* Ed. Rand J. Spiro, Bertram C. Bruce, and William F. Brewer, 279–307. Hillsdale: Erlbaum, 1980.

Nelson, Jennie, and John R. Hayes. "The Road Not Taken: How The Writing Context Influences Students' Choices." Paper read at the Conference on College Composition and Commmunication, St. Louis, 1988.

Nelson, Katherine. "Cognitive Development and the Acquisition of Concepts." In *Schooling and the Acquisition of Knowledge*. Ed. Richard C. Anderson, Rand J. Spiro, and William E. Montague, 215–39. Hillsdale: Erlbaum, 1977.

North, Stephen. "Teaching Research Writing: Five Criteria." *Freshman English News, 9* (1980): 17–19.

Oakeshott, Michael. "The Voice of Poetry in the Conversation of Mankind." In *Rationalism in Politics and Other Essays*, 197–247. London: Methuen, 1962.

Pappas, Christine C. "The Role of 'Typicality' in Reading Comprehension." In *Understanding Readers' Understanding: Theory and Practice*. Ed. Robert J. Tierney, Patricia L. Anders, and Judy Nichols Mitchell, 129–45. Hillsdale: Erlbaum, 1987.

Perelman, Chaim, and L. Olbrechts-Tyteca. *The New Rhetoric: A Treatise on Argumentation*. Trans. John Wilkinson and Purcell Weaver. Notre Dame: University of Notre Dame Press, 1969.

Piaget, Jean, and Barbel Inhelder. *The Psychology of the Child*. Trans. Helen Weaver. New York: Basic, 1969.

Plato. *Gorgias*. Trans. W. C. Helmbold. Indianapolis: Bobbs-Merrill, 1952.

———. *Phaedrus*. Trans. W. C. Helmbold and W. G. Rabinowitz. Indianapolis: Bobbs-Merrill, 1956.

Polanyi, Michael. *Personal Knowledge: Towards a Post-Critical Philosophy*. Chicago: University of Chicago Press, 1958.

Pratt, Mary Louise. *Toward a Speech-Act Theory of Literary Discourse*. Bloomington: Indiana University Press, 1977.

Reither, James A. "Writing and Knowing: Toward Redefining the Writing Process." *College English, 47* (1985): 620–28.

Reither, James A., and Douglas Vipond. "Writing as Collaboration." *College English, 51* (1989): 855–67.

Rosenblatt, Louise. *The Reader, The Text, The Poem: The Transactional Theory of the Literary Work*. Carbondale: Southern Illinois University Press, 1978.

Rosch, Eleanor. "Universals and Cultural Specifics in Human Categorization." In *Cross-Cultural Perspectives on Learning*. Ed. Richard W. Brislin, Stephen Bochner, Walker J. Lonner, 177–206. New York: Sage-Wiley, 1975.

Rosch, Eleanor, et al. "Basic Objects in Natural Categories." *Cognitive Psychology, 8* (1976): 382–439.

Rumelhart, David E. "Schemata: The Building Blocks of Cognition." In *Theoretical Issues in Reading Comprehension: Perspectives from Cognitive Psychology, Linguistics, Artificial Intelligence, and Education*. Ed. Rand J. Spiro, Bertram C. Bruce, and William F. Brewer, 33–58. Hillsdale: Erlbaum, 1980.

Rumelhart, David E., and Andrew Ortony. "The Representation of Knowledge in Memory." In *Schooling and the Acquisition of Knowledge*. Ed. Richard C. Anderson, Rand J. Spiro, and William E. Montague, 99–135. Hillsdale: Erlbaum, 1977.

Shank, Roger, and Robert Abelson. *Scripts, Plans, Goals and Understanding*. Hillsdale: Erlbaum, 1977.

Scholes, Robert. *Protocols of Reading*. New Haven: Yale University Press, 1989.

———. *Textual Power: Literary Theory and the Teaching of English*. New Haven: Yale University Press, 1985.

Smith, Frank. *Understanding Reading: A Psycholinguistic Analysis of Reading and Learning to Read.* 2nd ed. New York: Holt, 1978.

Sperber, Dan, and Deirdre Wilson. *Relevance: Communication and Cognition.* Cambridge: Harvard University Press, 1986.

Spiro, Rand J. "Constructive Processes in Prose Comprehension and Recall." In *Theoretical Issues in Reading Comprehension: Perspectives from Cognitive Psychology, Linguistics, Artificial Intelligence, and Education.* Ed. Rand J. Spiro, Bertram C. Bruce, and William F. Brewer, 245–78. Hillsdale: Erlbaum, 1980.

———. "Remembering Information from Text: The 'State of Schema' Approach." In *Schooling and the Acquisition of Knowledge.* Ed. Richard C. Anderson, Rand J. Spiro, and William E. Montague, 137–65. Hillsdale: Erlbaum, 1977.

Spivey, Nancy Nelson. "Construing Constructivism: Reading Research in the United States." *Poetics,* 16 (1987): 169–92.

Trimbur, John. "Consensus and Difference in Collaborative Learning." *College English,* 51 (1989): 602–16.

van Dijk, Teun A. "Relevance Assignment in Discourse Production." *Discourse Processes,* 2 (1979): 113–26.

van Dijk, Teun A., and Walter Kintsch. *Strategies of Discourse Comprehension.* New York: Academic, 1983.

Vygotsky, Lev Semenovitch. *Thought and Language.* Ed. and Trans. Eugenia Hanfmann and Gertrude Vakar. Cambridge: MIT, 1962.

Weaver, Richard M. "Language is Sermonic." In *Language is Sermonic: Richard M. Weaver on the Nature of Rhetoric.* Ed. Richard L. Johannesen, Rennard Strickland, and Ralph T. Eubanks, 201–25. Baton Rouge: Louisiana State University Press, 1970.

———. "Ultimate Terms in Contemporary Rhetoric." In *Language is Sermonic: Richard M. Weaver on the Nature of Rhetoric.* Ed. Richard L. Johannesen, Rennard Strickland, and Ralph T. Eubanks, 87–122. Baton Rouge: Louisiana State University Press, 1970.

Wells, David M. "A Program for the Freshman Research Paper." *College Composition and Communication,* 28 (1977): 383–84.

Whately, Richard. *Elements of Rhetoric.* Ed. Douglas Ehninger. Carbondale: Southern Illinois University Press, 1963.

Wyer, Robert S. "Attitudes, Beliefs, and Information Acquisition." In *Schooling and the Acquisition of Knowledge.* Ed. Richard C. Anderson, Rand J. Spiro, and William E. Montague, 259–88. Hillsdale: Erlbaum, 1977.

Young, Richard. "Arts, Crafts, Gifts and Knacks: Some Disharmonies in the New Rhetoric." In *Reinventing the Rhetorical Tradition.* Ed. Aviva Freedman and Ian Pringle, 53–60. Ottawa: Canadian Council of Teachers of English, 1980.

Young, Richard, Alton L. Becker, and Kenneth L. Pike. *Rhetoric: Discovery and Change.* New York: Harcourt, 1970.

Index

Author

Doug Brent is assistant professor in the inter-disciplinary faculty of general studies at the University of Calgary, Canada. He teaches a broad range of courses in the field of communications studies, ranging from tutorials for beginning writers through advanced courses in history and theory of rhetoric, history of communications, and computers and society. His articles have appeared in journals such as *College English,* the *Journal of Business Communications,* and *The Writing Instructor,* and he is a consulting editor of *Ejournal,* an electronic journal concerned with the implications of electronic documents and networks. He is currently researching the rhetorical implications of William Perry's theories of intellectual development.